IN THE WORLD'S ATTIC

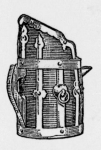

STEEL BOUND WOOD
CHANG JUG.

SUCH SUBLIME VISTAS! SUCH LIGHTS ON FAR OFF PEAKS WHERE
A BEND OF THE ROAD OPENED A WIDER VIEW.

IN THE WORLD'S ATTIC

BY

HENRIETTA SANDS MERRICK

INTRODUCTION BY

SIR FRANCIS YOUNGHUSBAND

K.C.S.I., K.C.I.E., C.I.E.

"Somebody once described Ladakh as being, if not
the 'Roof of the World'—a term generally applied to
the Pamirs—as 'at least the attic.' But I think more
correctly Ladakh could lay claim to being the actual
roof."
MAJOR M. L. A. GOMPERTY in "Magic Ladakh."

66 ILLUSTRATIONS
FROM PHOTOGRAPHS BY THE AUTHOR
COLOUR PRINTS BY MRS. A. E. BERRY

NEW YORK : LONDON
G. P. PUTNAM'S SONS
The Knickerbocker Press
1931

Made in the United States of America

5370

TO DICK

In memory

white man's foot had ever before reached . . . where none has trodden since. Where not even a native had passed in twenty-five years. He was attempting to find a way into India across the long-disused Mustagh Pass that divides Chinese Turkestan from the British dependencies. He had no mountaineering experience . . . none of the proper appliances for mountain climbing. His boots were without nails and when they wore out on glacier rock he went on in soleless leather socks. When these in turn were torn to pieces he dragged bleeding feet across the ice and snow.

Weak from climbing at such high altitudes, hungry, and frozen, he let himself down over the precipice of rock and ice and snow where there was no sure foothold or handhold and then for days followed down one of the greatest glaciers in the world . . . the Baltoro, and on into Askoli in Baltistan. He had completed a journey of nearly four thousand miles from Peking to India and had recorded the greatest romance of the day.

That boy, Francis Younghusband, was in 1904 the leader of the British Mission to Lhasa which made possible the expedition which I am at present preparing into Tibet. He is now a veteran, loaded with honours from his King and from his country. I am proud to be able to express my appreciation of his graciousness in writing the introduction to my effort to describe what was to me a great undertaking among the high snows yet which to him must read like a child's tale.

My thanks are due also to Mr. J. G. Acheson, Deputy Secretary to the Government of India, for having opened the gates for me that led to this adventure. And to the British Joint Commissioner for Ladakh, Captain G. A. Falconer, for having granted me the necessary permit for the expedition. I also want to thank him and Mrs. Falconer and also Bishop Peter of Leh for their many courtesies.

I am particularly indebted to Colonel A. E. Berry for his kindness and helpfulness. And to Mrs. Berry for having made for me the water colour sketches that add so much to the interest of this book.

For having read and criticised the manuscript I am sincerely grateful to my instructor at Columbia University, Professor Dorothy Scarborough, to Mrs. B. G. du Pont, and to Madame Margharita Derfelden. And to Mrs. George Randolph Kantzler for having secured for me the quiet spot where I could finish the work.

Last, but not least, is my gratitude to Gulam, my faithful Ladakhi servant who cooked my food, pitched my tents, slept across my doorway to protect me, and who guided me on the long journey of two hundred and fifty miles across the Himalaya back to civilization.

H. S. M.

DARJEELING,
March 21, 1931.

INTRODUCTION

IF the writer of an introduction to a book should be as cold and impartial as a judge, I am no fit and proper person to introduce this book. For I am grossly and unabashedly partial. I am too much in love with the Himalaya to be anything else. Moreover, the book deals with my own particular part of the Himalaya. Moreover, again, I was handed the manuscript on a foggy, dreary day in London, when I had already suffered from four months of dreary, foggy London. So how could my heart help going out to the book, and how could I keep myself from it till I had read it through from first page to last?

And what are my impressions? First, that I must revise my opinion about the wisdom of the powers that be. Why is it that all the spirit of a great explorer, all the delight in achieving high altitudes, in wandering in wild places and vast expanses, and in overcoming tough obstacles, and all the capacity for leading men and carrying them along on great enterprises should be put into the frail body of a delicate woman, while many a hulking man goes about the world without a spark of spirit in him, perfectly content to oscillate backwards and forwards between his office desk and his home day after day and year after year? Whoever in the Universe is responsible for this—it seemed to me as I finished the reading—was about as worthy of our esteem as those who put larks into cages and let sheep go free.

Mrs. Merrick has made no new exploration. But what she has done is to go over old tracks in a new spirit. Who would not like to re-capture his childhood's delight in every new adventure, to experience once more the eager expectation of wonders that will surely open up, to know again the thrill of dangers ahead? She has shown with the fresh innocence of a child what the blasé traveller fails to note for the benefit of his fellows, the joys that the Himalaya can afford, even in its well-known parts.

Also she has made the people live in her pages. There we can see them exactly the same today as they were when I knew them forty years ago. The importunate Kashmiris clamouring for service as soon as the word goes round the bazaar that servants are required. The same old devices. The same summary dismissal when the devices are discovered by the enraged employer. And the same devoted service by the one who is eventually chosen.

And then at the far end of the journey the happy-go-lucky, cheery, affectionate Ladakhis. None of these has changed. And one is grateful for Mrs. Merrick's gently sympathetic nature which enabled her to draw these people out and make us understand them.

One only regret I have about the book is that she could not find more opportunity for that long silent commune with the great mountains and the still solitudes and the starry firmament that we can feel her soul was craving for. Only once or twice had she a fleeting chance. And of each she made the most. Yet, when so sensitive a spirit had at such bodily cost made her way into those great vastnesses, one feels sorry that she could not have remained in untrammelled peace to take in the full measure of their mighty influence.

In any case she has shown that the Himalaya is accessible even to the town-bred and the inexperienced if only they have the pluck and enterprise. Some people seem to feel only depressed and overcome by great mountains. Their magnitude only fills them with a sense of their own insignificance in comparison. Such had better stay away. The Himalaya is no fitting place for them. But others there are who feel their whole being drawn out by the sight of the pure and lofty summit of some Himalayan monarch. And they experience a joy which lasts them all their lives. To them for always after the world is something greater than it had ever been before. They see richer possibilities and fuller glories. And it is such as these that Mrs. Merrick's book may draw to the Himalaya. May there be many of them. And may I add that the full glory of the mountains is only revealed to those who win it by their own exertions.

Francis Younghusband

PREFACE

AMERICANS are travelling to India in increasing numbers each year. Most of them dash through it, "toured" by an agency, in what is rarely the good season for travel there.

Kashmir is taken in by a few venturesome tourists as a side trip, a week at most allotted to it, and this rarely in the month of May when Srinagar is at its best.

Few people in America realize how accessible India is, nor how easy and how cheap it is to travel and to live there. They do not know how comfortable one can be for the months of the hot season when it is possible to go "off into the blue" fishing, hunting, trekking . . . or just loafing in tent or houseboat or "hut" in the glorious mountains, with abundant food and willing service. And at a cost that is within the reach of an humble bank account.

This book describes one of the many fascinating ways of travelling de luxe on a mere shoe-string.

When the inspiration to make the strange trip to Leh came to me I assembled all of the available literature on the subject. No one book gave the picture of its weird grandeur as well as the practical things that a traveller must know . . . clothes, equipment, food, servants, costs. These will remain the same for many years to come. I have given in an appendix, for the benefit of those who can make the trip, such details as would break the narrative of a beauty that I have tried to share with the unfortunate ones who cannot.

Across one of the five worst passes in the whole range of the Himalayas, down into what is said to be the world's deepest gorge, along narrow rock shelves, and fording rivers, the road to Leh leads away from the crowd into the vast spaces of a new world.

If a woman so ill-equipped for such a trip as I was, could make it, it would be feasible for anyone who had the foresight to secure the necessary and scarce permits from the British Joint Commissioner for Ladakh at Srinagar in Kashmir.

H. S. M.

NEW YORK,
September 1931.

BRASS BOUND WOODEN
TEA POT FROM A
LAMASERY.

MANÉ STONE.

CONTENTS

xvii

CONTENTS

COPPER HOLY WATER PITCHER.

HAND WROUGHT
STIRRUP FROM
LHASSA.

ILLUSTRATIONS

xix

ILLUSTRATIONS xxi

IN THE WORLD'S ATTIC

PRAYER STONE CARVED WITH
THE MANTRA OF TIBET,
"OM MANÈ PADME HUM."

IN THE WORLD'S ATTIC

CHAPTER I

THE CALL OF THE UNKNOWN

Across the Himalayas! Not even the edge of my dreams had touched those far-flung horizons until spring found me lotus-eating in the beautiful "Vale of Kashmir" after a year of wandering.

Iceland and the North Cape; Norway's Fjords ... like Judgment Day incarnate; Sweden, France and Italy ... even the crater of Vesuvius was full of tourists. Their silhouettes broke vistas of glorious sunsets on the Nile ... crowded out the Sphinx's mystery.

When Robert Hichens came to tea with me in Luxor I asked him: "Where is the desert's solitude?"

He told me how he crossed the Nile and rode the wastes of sand.

India was less accessible.

Going to India was like throwing off a yoke.

3

And there I wandered over ten thousand miles alone with my Hindu bearer.

I visited fairy white palaces floating in a peaceful lake. I climbed high to alabaster temples where flowers of fretwork dropped from ceilings like rose point lace. I strolled through zenanas where encrusted mirrors sparkled like a million diamonds.

I saw the Taj by day and the Taj by night . . . my bearer excluded from the garden that his footsteps might not break the enchanted stillness.

We went to Greek cities . . . rising from the dead. To the Towers of Silence. Even for a tiger hunt in the jungles of Bengal. There were nights in palaces and nights spent in station waiting rooms . . . my bearer sleeping across the barred doorway for my protection.

The Bazaars were masses of vivid colour, seething crowds . . . a mixture of animals and men. Sadhus, naked and smeared with ashes, held out begging bowls. Snake charmers played their flutes before writhing reptiles. Men, unheeded, bowed to the earth in prayer.

I knew the drone of street calls. Filth. Heat. Sweat. And the maddening smell of human flesh!

Eyes were conspicuous everywhere. Eyes full of Fate! They looked at one across a gulf that one could not bridge. Sometimes they held a dangerous glitter . . . I moved on faster. Mostly they were indifferent, appraising the stranger who was but a passing footstep on the sands.

Temples reeked with rancid butter that bespattered monstrous Gods of stone. Garlands encircled emblems of Siva and Parvati. Foreheads were painted with like symbols. There were vestiges of drying blood.

India holds an open sore in one hand . . . and balm in the other.

In spite of sordidness and filth, degenerate worship, India is spiritual. One feels it everywhere. It is deep down.

India is like a fever.

Riots both religious and political stressed the uncertainty of everything. Blood feuds raged along the northwest frontier. War in Afghanistan was uncomfortably near, when I crossed the Khyber and the Kohat Passes. Strain and tension were on every side like hot jungle breath.

A mounting thermometer drove me from the plains . . . Kashmir was like a cool hand on my forehead. It is called "The Happy Valley" and is tucked away in the northwest corner of India girdled by the Hindu Kush and Himalayas. A few years ago it took three weeks to drive in from Rawal Pindi where the railroad stops. I reached it in ten hours . . . speeding across the glorious mountains in an automobile.

Kashmir is like rest when the day's work is done.

There I led a life of complete idleness. Day after day I lay back among the red-embroidered cushions of my "shikara" while the boatmen plied their heart-shaped oars along the Jhelum River where fragrant bushes dip their blossoms into the water and banks run up to meet fields of mustard. Sometimes we sped across the waters of Lak Dal to some pleasure garden of the Great Moghuls. On every side the towering snow peaks of the Himalayas encircled the "Happy Valley" as if to shut off that bit of Paradise from the turmoil of the rest of the world.

Gliding among lotus leaves uptilted in the breeze I landed at Nishat Bagh, "The Garden of Gladness," and loafed the morning away prone on a carpet of tiny pink and white English daisies watching the bright waters cascade down ten flower-decked terraces to Lak Dal.

On other days the Shalimar, "The Abode of Love," saw my "shikara" moored for long hours beneath its walls while I wandered where once the beautiful Nourmahal, "Light of the Harem," of Jehangir, laughed and loved and danced beside the same fountains that played for me. Surely they sang: "Pale hands I loved beside the Shalimar. Where are you now . . . ?"

And there in the black granite pavilion where

Lalla Rookh with fingers henna-dyed and rose-coloured bridal veil floating on the breeze came to her nuptial feast, I feasted too, wondering the while if it was she who had had engraved on one of the columns: "If there be an Elysium on Earth it is this, it is this." So peaceful and so still is the Shalimar that the fluttering of birds' wings in the water and the rustling of "chenar" leaves are a break in the silence.

From the roof of my houseboat I saw the days slip down among the yesterdays, far peaks paling into purple shadows only to rend the sky at dawn, hemming me in, limiting me to memories perhaps too bitter sweet. Months of suspended living lay ahead while the plains of India sizzled in a heat too grilling to be dared, and for all of its hypnotic beauty I began to feel that the flowers merely hid the bars of a cage.

I wanted to get away, to end days of dreaming under the spreading branches of "chenars" in Asoka's "Garden of Bliss"; away from the mountains that looked down on me as I so often looked down from the "Takht-i-Suleiman," the "Seat of Solomon," on its high hill above Srinagar to where the Jhelum wound its shawl pattern among the fields and where Lak Dal lay placid as a dewdrop on the petal of a rose.

I was told of a remoter garden and I clambered

up banks where sweet William, fuchsia, coryopsis
and gallardia, Canterbury bells and foxglove vied
in beauty with a bush of "Gloire de Dijon" flaunt-
ing just one pink rose among its matchless yellow
buds.

There behind high walls lay the Chasma Shahi
or Giant Fountain, its waters gushing up through
a black marble funnel, cool, tonic and refreshing.
Minas flitted fearlessly about; the dappled yellow
hoopoe spread its lovely crest and bulbuls of olive-
yellow looked at me knowingly with their wicked
yellow eyes. Beyond my retreat spread fields of
linseed just budding into blue where wild forget-
me-nots mingled with purple vetch. The sky was
overcast but when the veil of mist was rent, giant
snow clad peaks once more bounded my horizon.

I could not get away from those fingers pointing
into the unknown. What hid beyond them? Was
there any reality in the vast peace that lay upon
the "Happy Valley" or was it illusion and was
reality up there in those mysteries of snow?

Steeped in the beauty of the land of lotus flowers, I fed my spirit with tales I had read of the
wild mountains. I recalled the exploits of a mere
boy who had for years been my hero . . . Francis
Younghusband, who had passed where never before had the foot of a white man trod, and never
since! And I read of the experiences of Major

Blacker of the Guides along the roof of the world where I could never venture. If only I could be like:

"... l'oiseau posé pour un instant sur des rameaux
     trop frèles,
Qui sent ployer la branche et qui chante pourtant
Sachant qu'il a des ailes!"

But only eagles winged so high!

Then I learned that regular trade routes crossed those barriers of snow and the thought of them became an obsession with me. One such route ran north to Gilgit where Nanga Parbat, 26,620 feet high, could best be seen, and from there carried on to Kashgar. A branch led off to Yarkand, and in a curve struck down across the Karakorum range into Leh in Ladakh, then turned back along the Indus River into Kashmir.

Major Gompertz in "Magic Ladakh" pointed this route that seemed more possible. Even such as I might make it, though people said of it that if not the roof of the world it was certainly the attic. I should like to explore the world's attic!

Inquiry revealed that each year only twenty-four passes were granted for the trip. But, armed with a letter of introduction from Mr. Acheson, Deputy Secretary for the Government of India, whom I had met in Delhi, I applied to the

British Joint Commissioner for Ladakh for two permits, hoping to find someone to accompany me.

His reply informed me that the season for visiting Ladakh was divided into two periods: The first one was from April 15th, when the passes are officially declared open, until July 15th; and the second from July 15th to October 15th, when the passes are once more closed with snow. Captain Falconer, the British Joint Commissioner, told me also that the twelve permits for the first period having been issued, my name was noted as fifth and sixth on the Waiting List and provisionally entered for the second period. Permits would be issued to me before I actually started, if I would call for them at the Residency Office.

Only the hardiest break the barriers of snow in April, but from the end of May to the middle of July is the most desirable time for the trip, the second period falling during flood season when landslides are more to be feared, when bridges are washed away, and when, at an altitude that offers little protection from dangerous violet rays, one is exposed to the pitiless August sun through long stretches of desert. Because of the difficulty of getting supplies and transport the rule governing these periods is rigid and I had to content myself with the hope that some one who had permits for the first one would drop out. I was listed to go, however, and from then on the days became just preparations for the trip.

That part of the Central Asian Highway I was to travel is inaccessible to wheel traffic, a mere camel track in places and mostly just rock ledge cut along the face of cliffs or tracks through desert wastes. For six months of the year it is closed to man and beast by barriers of snow, but leads on to the highest capital city in the world—Leh in Ladakh, lying at eleven thousand five hundred feet. Ladakh, often spoken of as "Little Tibet" and once a part of Greater Tibet, was conquered in 1848 by the Dogra General of Jammu, and since then has been the property of the Dogra Kings. When the Dogra King of Jammu, Gulab Sing, bought Kashmir from the British, Ladakh became a province of Kashmir, and it is governed by the Maharaja of Kashmir represented by a Wazir, and by the British Joint Commissioner, who together keep the road open.

What visions of those wild and lonely stretches beyond the high ranges came to me! My life had been lived at sea level, among the canyons of big American cities. I had never done any trekking. Though I boasted a hardy constitution several bouts with illness had left me with little enough strength for ordinary requirements and at that time I weighed only ninety-four pounds. Doubts and fears assailed me with the realization of what the years and all that goes to make up living had taken of my strength.

Deserts to cross, and in August heat!

Altitudes of over thirteen thousand feet that must be reached.

Long treks on foot!

And worst of all! The vision of myself on horse-back climbing up and down rock ladders zigzag on the face of sheer cliffs or along narrow rock cuttings one half of me hanging over a precipice. For that was the picture which books and people gave of the road.

All my life I have been desperately afraid of horses. The nearest I had come to mounting one was the purchase of riding habit and boots. But that was to please the one I lived to please, and for myself I was glad that illness prevented my ever getting beyond having a snap-shot taken in Gramercy Park, one foot resting carelessly, as it were, on a low rail while I grasped a newly purchased riding crop in one hand with what I thought to be the proper degree of nonchalance for an experienced horsewoman.

From the moment that I was enlisted for the trip to Leh life became a struggle to make my too rebellious body into a fitter instrument. First came a visit to the Kashmir Nursing Home, the local hospital, with petitions to the doctor in charge for every known strength-building tonic and food. My houseboat was a gymnasium where I tumbled about, improvising contortions to stretch muscles that even in my heyday had never been required to do more than carry me a few blocks along city streets or over a ballroom floor.

And horseback! Everyone said: "Get a horse and begin to ride or you'll never be able to stand the trip."

"Get a horse!" It sounded easy. Daily I watched those charming Englishwomen on their superb mounts, and nowhere does an English-woman show to such advantage; nowhere, unless it be when she graciously serves tea in her "shikara" that is drawn in between the floating gardens of Lak Dal and you lean back among the cushions and listen to the gentle inflexion of her voice and love the long oval of her face with its transparent skin and the flash of her white teeth, and bask in the calm she radiates. But her splendid mounts were not for me.

Srinagar is a small place so that everyone's affairs are market gossip and no sooner had some-one said: "Get a horse!" than horses began to appear like magic each day on the embankment above my houseboat. Lady B——'s "syce" brought a pretty animal but his letter of introduction

announced that he was named "Firefly." Had he
been called "Fido" I should have kept him. I had
my bearer pass the word that what I really wanted
was something more like a nice quiet cow, and
finally "Lalla" appeared, hanging his head as if
the gossip of the market place had reached him.
He was accepted forthwith to the tune of rupees
forty (eleven dollars) a month, including his keep,
and he proved to be as stubborn as I am myself.

But having got a horse, what was I to do with
him? Ride him along roads where automobiles
whizzed by and big lorries honked at every turn?
Not much! The quandary was solved by my meeting an expert riding teacher, an alluring young
woman of nine years. To call her a child would be
patronizing Veronica, daughter of an Army officer, who took her fences like a veteran, and who
consented to teach me exactly where between the
head and the tail of Lalla I should properly remain, and the touch of which rein or of which heel
would make Lalla go which way. This proved to
be an accumulation of useless knowledge, for on
the road I found that the only rein most ponies
in those regions know is a rope attached to their
halter. And my efforts at control or persuasion
were futile when I tried to coax them away from
the extreme edge of a rock ledge, the only response
being the turning of a long thin neck while hind

quarters curved more perilously near the edge. Who was I to dispute the instinct of generations backed by personal experience of the danger of striking packs against the rock walls rising on the inside of the path?

But all of this I did not know the while Veronica explained the mysteries of trot and canter and I begged off after a few rounds inside the mud enclosure where she taught me. I disgraced her, and I'm sure she was as delighted as was I when hotter weather drove me higher up in the mountains to a "hut" at Gulmarg at nine thousand feet. And with me I took another Lalla. Every horse now had that name which means, not "horse" in Hindustani, or even an index to its gender, but merely that the genus "syce" completely lacks imagination. My acquisition of the second Lalla came about in this way:

One of my charming English acquaintances asked a friend to look for a suitable mount for a scared-to-death woman and he sent word that such a beast was to be found out near his camp if I would come out and inspect it. I wrote asking that he put it in a cardboard box and send it in to me, but he insisted that I come out and interview it—so I went. I recognized its head from its tail at once when I saw it moving and when Lalla let me ride him into a tree without protest I thought he was admirably suited to my needs and sent him up to Gulmarg. Alas, it was the wisdom of old age that made him adjust to my humours. He proved unequal to the thousand foot climb to Killenmarg so I sent him back all newly shod at rupees one (thirty-seven cents) a hoof and with a sack of grain which I feel sure was eaten on the road back by the "syce" himself.

Lalla's trousseau, however, proved interesting. Someone advised that I would need a crupper to hold on to as I rode down steep slopes; another told me that a breast strap was essential to keep the saddle from slipping over his tail as I climbed rock ladders; furthermore I was told to take my own girths. So I went to the local supply man and said: "Give me his whole wardrobe." It came in due time. The breast strap fitted only two horses along the road and had to be discarded for another one; the crupper was too small, and the girth buckles broke half way to Leh so that thereafter my saddle was tied on with native ropes woven of "yak's" hair.

I had just got Lalla trained to come to the window of my hut to be fed over the sill, and all silky from brushing, and was about to train him to loll gracefully before my log fire when his infirmities necessitated his departure. And after all I made the trip on the ponies that were brought in at dawn each day, not at all comforted by those who tried to reassure me by saying: "Those hill ponies are like cats. You just sit on them and they'll take you anywhere." I didn't want to leap up and down sharp inclines or along rock ledges and I took little stock in their sure-footedness, as all accounts of the trip I had read spoke of the number of ponies that fell over those dread "khuds."

My attention was called to the fact that a horse had four legs, which did not convince me of their safety as they seemed to me just two extra encumbrances to slip with. And so it proved when my Lalla went down on an ice ledge crossing the Zoji-Là and nearly rolled over the side onto a snow bed while I, digging in my iron-tipped khud stick and hobnailed boots at every step, crossed without mishap.

But who in all that lovely valley had actually been to Leh and could tell me what clothes and equipment to take? I knew few people; was one of those queer wandering Americans who turn up in unexpected places and are neither tourists nor yet residents. My mountains had been crossed in trains, my duck-shooting days in Canada and the United States had called for little preparation, and I was now faced with the problem of making up so formidable a thing as a "bandobast." This is pronounced "bundobust" and means "arrange-ment" and stands for the whole outfit—equipment, food, servants, ponies and prices. And as every-one in Srinagar is making a bandobast of some sort it is the most frequently spoken word there. And so I was to make a bandobast and was en-chanted; but never having made one before I was at a loss how to proceed.

The British Joint Commissioner had only re-cently taken over his post and had never made the trip, and of the people going in he mentioned Colonel A. E. Berry, retired from the Indian Medical Service, who had been assigned by the British Government to go to Leh to care for the sick in Ladakh. I wrote him:

"Will you see an American woman who is going to Leh and knows nothing about it and give her some advice?"

A prompt answer was followed by a call and I gleaned my first authentic information about the requirements of the trip. It will sound like mere advice to you—but to me it was a whole symphony of marvels.

Distances on the road were measured not in miles but by "stages," each stage being the approx-imate limit of a man's endurance for the day, and at each stage was a dak bungalow, usually accom-

modating only two people. If no one else was in
quarters one could find shelter there unless one
preferred to pitch one's tent, which sometimes was
preferable. I gathered that to "faire la chasse
aux poux" was a sport of the road and was sure
of it when germicidal soap and Keating's powder
and Flit were advised as adjuncts to my outfit.
There should be also quinine, aspirin, Eno's fruit
salts, castor oil, eye wash, three inch bandages,
absorbent cotton, adhesive tape, peroxide, iodine,
cough mixture, and potass of permanganate. To
these, I added on other advice: boric vaseline,
chlorodyne, calomel and a mixture to cure sand-
fly bites, made of one part oil of cassia, two parts
brown oil of camphor and 4-5 parts vaseline. If
it did not cure the sand-fly bites that soon covered
every exposed inch of me it certainly distracted
me from all thought of them or anything else but
Hell Fire. I recalled Eben Holden's saying: "A
certain amount of fleas is good for a dog; it keeps
him from broodin' on bein' a dog."

Stress was laid on the importance of seeing that
all drinking water was boiled along the road as
streams were infected and also full of mica. Water
after boiling should be left to settle and only the
top used for cooking or drinking, as mica gives
colitis.

"You will carry a water bottle, of course," Colonel Berry said: "Between Gund and Sonamarg, after you pass Gagangir and before entering the Gorge you will see a stream coming out of the rocks. Fill your water bottle there. One mile from Baltal there is a spring below the road. Fill there as Baltal has no decent water. At Matayan there is a spring about six hundred yards away. Ask the 'chowkidar' where it is." And, by the way, a spring is called "chasma" in Urdu, but in Ladakhi it is "chimick." And so on the tale unfolded into ever greater mystery.

For clothes, I should have hobnailed boots or "chaplies" and "gilgits" if going in cold weather, these being a combination of leather and wool lined with lamb's wool. At any season a sweater would be needed for the start which should be made at dawn in order to cover as much of the road as possible while it was cool. A topi, or pith helmet, was of course essential and should be worn even in cloudy weather for violet rays in that thin air were dangerous. Also in a country where filth was universal, sanitary arrangements non-existent, and streams necessarily infected, it was important to guard against open sores and to care promptly for blisters.

All the necessary money for the trip out and back must be taken, preferably in denominations of one, two, four and eight annas as no change could be got along the road; and I should in person place the regulation amount in the hand of each coolie and pony man each day or claims would be made and trouble ensue.

Between gymnastics and walks I began to collect my outfit, and not knowing whether I might go in the first and colder period or in the second, I outfitted for both, having had some experience with Kashmiri procrastination. It sounds extravagant until you learn that coat and knickers of wool completely lined with lamb's wool cost rupees sixty or about twenty-two dollars. I did not take them with me, as I went in the second period after all, and I found that a three-piece homespun suit and one of sunproof khaki, which is a soft material woven red on one side, answered my needs. Red gives the greatest protection from violet rays and women in India often wear pieces of red flannel in the crown of their hats when they do not wear a topi.

And because a topi was necessary, and because I am an extremist, like the sun, I took in addition to my ordinary topi worn everywhere in India a "Mespot" topi that derived its name from having been the equipment of the soldiers in Mesopotamia during the war. It is made of one inch thick pith covered with quilted khaki, and is ugly on man or woman, though I never saw any other woman wear one. To mine I added a circular shield of khaki that fell to the shoulders and was carried in my pocket when not in use. It was easily slipped over the crown of my topi when the sun got too hot on the back of my neck. I had it copied in Peshawar from a photograph of Lowell Thomas in his book "Beyond Khyber Pass."

Beneath my coat I wore a thin spine pad of cork, khaki covered. Add dark goggles closed in at the sides and you have the picture that would put all the gargoyles on church steeples to shame. I was taking no chances with the burning sun of July and August, having a head that stood even moderate heat too ill after brain fever and later sunstroke. And I thanked my stars for all the precautions as I swayed in my saddle from dizziness through the long desert treks.

There were woollen gloves and stockings besides, both badly needed, and shirtwaists, and fur-lined sleeping socks that came above my knees and saved my life when a cold wind howled around my tent. And I had boots made at the native shops and also "chaplies." I tried to achieve a pair of jodhpurs, so easily slipped on when you rise in the dark and dress by candlelight. But almost every shop in Kashmir retains a pair of my nearly-but-not-quite-fitting ones, and I was forced to ride forth in breeches that at least left plenty of room for woolies beneath, plus the pad that I preferred to put there instead of on my saddle.

Within a few hours of my first purchase every shopman knew that I was going to Leh. Was I not the fabulously rich American "mem-sahib" who could afford to order three suits at once? Were not all Americans rich and therefore fair game for a poor merchant who must make his little pile during the few summer months when visitors flocked to Kashmir? Every shopman urged me to take almost his entire stock to Leh, and when the rascal looked at me appealingly with soft eyes and called me "Hazoor," "The Presence," in plaintive tones it was difficult to resist doing so. Whether it was Mohamed Malik le Mar or Mohamed Baba, dressed all in white, his beard dyed red to show that he had been to Mecca, there was interesting bargaining about tubs and tent hooks and "yak-dans"; the latter I would have bought for the name alone even if they had not been beautiful boxes covered with cowhide and ornamented with straps and artistic metal hasps. Two of them held all my clothes and much besides.

As I intended to go beyond Leh if I ever got so far, and on over the Khardong Pass of the Karakorum range that leads on to Yarkand and Samarkand, and is 18,142 feet high, I sent to

Bombay for an altimeter and found that none could be procured in India that registered over fifteen thousand feet, a strange fact in a country that has the highest mountains in the world. I contented myself with a thermometer that recorded 240° Fahrenheit, and a pedometer that proved useless with the necessarily irregular paces of such a trek, for it was calibrated to 110 steps to 100 yards.

Early in the season I had secured a shikari-cook for the trip and with seemingly great trouble and corresponding demands for pay he had procured the other necessary servants for my outfit, a "bishti," or water carrier, and a sweeper.

The question of who should use my second permit bothered me not a little as women are not allowed to make the trip alone and everyone advised me to take a man with me in preference to another woman. I wanted to get the question settled at once so as not to be forced to give up the trip at the last moment and thought of a Mr. Phelps whom I had met down in India. I was then staying at Dean's Hotel in Peshawar. He heard that an American woman had ordered a motor to go across the Kohat Pass and declared that no woman should go there alone. It ran through tribal territory and a blood feud had just

broken out along the pass, which is more interesting than the Khyber.

I was delighted to have Mr. Phelps go with me
as he volunteered to do. I was still more pleased
when he did not try to make conversation in a
motor car, and thought that he would do for such
a trip as the one to Leh.

I wrote him that I had secured two of the scarce
permits for the trip and hoped that it would lure
him . . . that as I was asking for his protection to
Leh and back I wanted him to go as my guest. I
was delighted to get his telegram accepting in spite
of my avowal that I could not ride or swim and
was uncertain how I would stand the heat or altitude. His telegram was followed by a letter which
read: "The heat here is sanguinary. 112 today.
We killed a cobra in our house and caught a burglar the same night. We're wishing we'd killed the
burglar as well, as three of us have had to go to a
magistrate's court to give evidence."

The main problem of my trip was solved to the
satisfaction of the Joint Commissioner. But not
to that of the American Consul General in Calcutta to whom I confided my intentions plus the
list of my property to be shipped home, in the
event that . . .

A widely travelled lady, Mrs. Grundy might

take notice of even so inconspicuous a person as myself. Why feed her a tempting morsel?

By virtue of the fact that his cousin had married my cousin, Bob Frazer felt that he should argue points with this "relatively" distant connection in the interests of family and international relations. In my unapproved rambles alone throughout India he had more than once advised me: "Don't make yourself a nuisance to the British authorities." Now I had acted on the advice of such authority and he still disapproved of me.

"Then lend me an American Consul to go with me," I begged.

He preferred to keep them busy in the heat of Calcutta. I appealed to his sister to go along. Margaret would have none of it.

"That's all right for you and Byrd and Lindbergh," she wrote, "but I love my pipe and my carpet slippers too well."

It seemed hopeless. I wrote to Mr. Phelps:

"Is there another stray man or woman of your acquaintance who would go?"

Apparently there was not. Of the men he wrote:

"Isn't it odd? When you want a man there isn't one to be had; and when you particularly don't want even one they hang about in dozens and one dances only twice in the evening with one's girl friend."

Then Margaret came to the rescue:

"You'd be a fool not to go. It's an expedition and not a joy ride, and people look at things differently these days. You're too well known in your own circle and too little known up there to have what is said matter either way."

After all. Gossip . . . and the Himalayas . . . How incongruous!

I dismissed the thought and hoped only that I would not be too much of a nuisance to my escort. I consoled myself by appropriating the promise of Genesis: "And now nothing shall be restrained from them which they have imagined to do."

CHAPTER II

"TO THEM THAT HATH . . ."

BUT luck was with me.

One day as I was walking on the bund I met a woman whom I had seen several times in Calcutta. Red-haired, blue-eyed, she was with a figure one looked at twice. She was the widow of an Army officer who, like many met with in India, had returned to the land where living is cheap, friends plentiful, and patronage assured for such as are enterprising enough to import the latest French creations, or give the newest twist to one's "bob," or "bear-lead" some Maharani.

Mrs. Duncan came back to tiffin with me. She had only a few days to spend in Srinagar before going with friends who had their houseboat moored at one of the quiet spots on Lak Dal.

When she heard of my coming trek across the Himalayas she was so enthusiastic that I suggested that she join the expedition. Her acceptance solved the one remaining problem.

We spent the afternoon going over lists. I explained that Mr. Phelps and I wished to travel light. She demurred at a forty pound tent. I found myself engaged to take an eight by eight (which weighs about one hundred and fifty pounds) for each of us, and a ten by ten mess tent. It seemed superfluous to me, but the vision she conjured of desert heat, the shade of wide-spreading tent flies; plenty of room to move about in; shelter from cold winds at night . . . conquered my resistance.

"We'll be travelling 'à la Mogole,' as Bernier calls it," I exclaimed.

"What's the difference . . . we can get plenty of ponies," she countered.

Nothing made any difference to me so long as the early morning start was assured and she said she was as eager for it as was I.

She checked the list of supplies that Cockburn's Agency had made out for me. The only suggestion that Mr. Phelps had made was that I take some Bovril along. Impossible luxury in a country where the cow is sacred. The Maharaja prohibits even the importation of such sacrilegious stuff. We all agreed that Johnnie Walker would pack best for transportation.

Mrs. Duncan also reinstated the "bishti" whom Mr. Phelps had scratched as one man too many who would need to have food and equipment provided and carried.

There remained to announce Mrs. Duncan to Mr. Phelps. Would he balk at the responsibility of having two women to look out for?

"I hadn't time to consult you," I wrote. "She was leaving Srinagar in two days and had to know at once. Do save your fury until you've seen her. . . . Then you will bless me. She will cure the sore eyes that I shall give you."

What a relief when he wrote: "I'll be happy with anyone."

Mrs. Duncan departed. I was left to do all the work . . . which was interesting. I was making up a "bandobast."

But I also had some qualms.

Except for those met with in the Embassy circle in Washington, the home of my girlhood, I had seen little of English people until I went to India. I had sat under some of their lecturers who visit us occasionally and got the impression that they found it tedious to descend to the low mental level of their erstwhile colony. I did not look forward with any degree of pleasure to association with English people in India.

I was surprised to find them simple, kindly, and spontaneous as we ourselves rarely are with entire strangers who have no letters of introduction. They had gone out of their way to show me special courtesies and to smooth my path in many instances. I had found real companionship with the people of my blood. We even understood one another's brand of humour.

Yet memory flashed a searchlight on one unpleasant experience.

I once had a guest at my table in the hotel . . . an Englishman.

A woman, an acquaintance of his, joined us. She immediately absorbed him and when I tried to join in the conversation she fixed me with a faintly puzzled yet tolerant expression as if to say: "It's impossible to understand your incredible speech."

Sometimes she repeated my words . . . correcting my pronunciation: "Oh! . . . You mean . . . this or that, or so and so . . ."

It was difficult for me to repress a smile when she declared that she was more English than the English . . . then raised her glass and drank the young man's health . . . excluding me.

My sense of humour finally began to lag when she turned to him and drawled:

"Just fahncy! The other day I was taken for an American . . . An A-mer-i-can! Just fahncy!"

She gurgled the *r* . . . It was for all the world as if she had said: "A dino-saur-i-an."

I could not help saying to him:

"How could anyone make such a mistake! I

assure you we have nothing . . . nothing at all like her in America!"

Happily that had been a short experience . . . but this! Weeks and weeks with those who might flout me at my own table. The amazing thing had happened once . . . it might again. And I would be quite helpless off in the wilds with them . . .

But no! Why pit that one unpleasant hour against the many charming ones that had given me such cherished memories during the past eight months? Generous kindness! Freely offered help! Spontaneous friendships that had thrown open doors and said to the stranger: "Our home is yours."

I banished my fears. A charming letter came from Mrs. Duncan:

"You can't think how grateful I am for all the endless trouble you've taken. And I step in with all arrangements made for me. I'm sure it will be a success and I for my part will do all I possibly can to help you in every way."

Surely all would be well!

Time passed rapidly. There had to be a lot of correspondence with lists sent back and forth between the three of us. And with the prospect of another woman and her bearer to look out for the shikari-cook, whom I was keeping in my service,

began to give trouble. There was plenty to keep
me busy.

After exercising and arranging the details of
the trip I spent what time was left in reading, and
always about Himalayan passes . . . such irresist-
ible books as have been written by Colonel Younghusband, of which there are several, and by Major
Blacker of the Guides, Arthur Neve and Tyndale
Biscoe, and by Sven Hedin and Marco Polo. All
recording adventures in such high places as I was
going to and much of it about the very road.

Such things as Atmospheric Pressure became
interesting. I learned that at sea level it is 14.22
and on the Zoji-Là which I was to cross at eleven
thousand five hundred feet, it would be 9.83. At
fourteen thousand feet it would be 8.94. And only
8.44 at fifteen thousand feet. I expected to go
higher than that and did.

I was told also that at high altitudes the blood
was closer to the wall of the lungs and pneumonia
a thing to be guarded against. I found that precautions were also to be taken against cholera, and
I was inoculated for that, having already been
vaccinated for smallpox.

And what a land I was going to see! Wild as
the rivers that tore at its heart, rending frail
bridges by which men had to cross; lonely as the

mysterious land of which it once was part and to which it is still ethnographically and religiously bound, that land of Tibet which holds itself aloof from all the world in its valleys higher than the pinnacle of Mt. Blanc and three quarters of its entire area standing over ten thousand feet above sea level. No part of Ladakh to which I was going is below eight thousand feet. Perhaps a few passages from the books I read can best convey the picture that lured me on in spite of my dreads and fears.

Arthur Neve, who is the greatest authority on travel in Kashmir and the author of the only guide book to its passes, writes in his "Thirty Years in Kashmir" of his trip to Leh which also was made in July: "For several hundred miles there is no gap in the great snowy wall of the middle range of the Himalayas to the Zoji Pass or Zoji-Là. . . . This then is the main route from Northern India to Central Asia. . . . It crosses no less than seven snowy passes and forces its way onward in spite of the combined forces of nature; obstructed by land-slips and rocks, diverted by unfordable rivers; swept by avalanches; exposed to a tropical sun in shadeless ravines and to Arctic gales on shelterless plateaus. . . ."

Of the Zoji-Là itself he writes: "Many a trader's pony never gets across at all, for in wet weather the path is slippery, and a fall over the side is inevitably fatal." He describes the view from the top of the pass: "Then we turn north and realize that the waste of snow before us is the frontier of barren Tibet, where sandy plains replace verdant meadows and where the wild ridges jutting up against the sky are kept bare of vegetation, their strata crumbling under the destructive frost, snow and sun, leaving bare ribs of gaunt and often fantastic outline. There is ridge beyond ridge, wave after wave, each higher than the other and all culminating in the mighty masses of the Karakorum."

And Sven Hedin writes: "The road up the Zo-ji-Là is along a wall of rock—steep, treacherous. . . ."

I put down the books of great explorers and picked up a little volume written by a woman who had gone out with some missionaries. She writes of the Zoji Pass: "I looked up at the enormous cliffs encircling us as though we were insects at the base of a cup and wondered once more in all this narrow vertical world where was the outlet? Then I saw it. A path in zigzag, just two angles, cut in the face of a high green mountain straight before us. All very well there, but when it crept along the rocky edge . . . We reached the upper path, crawled round a nasty bit I had marked from far below where it bulged over, a sort of crusty bunion on the mountain side, got round a corner and, always mounting, came to a deep, dark rift or angle of the cliff, curving upward to a gigantic wall ahead, absolutely sheer, with a black thread, the path, sloping steeply up its face."

Nothing that I heard of the road encouraged me. And I should have to ride a horse across those rock ledges—that appalled me most of all! And once when I was in Cockburn's Agency looking over maps and discussing alternative routes for the home journey an officer who was engaged in tracing map routes over high snows asked if I were going to Leh. My affirmative he answered with the ejaculation:

"That's very sporting of you!"

This did not make me feel happier; it made me feel stupid, as if about to undertake an inevitable failure, for I was not hardening muscles fast enough and knew that I should never overcome my fear of horses or collect the necessary knee grip, and I still tired too quickly.

So from Cockburn's I turned in next door at Razaka's where I had found much that I needed for the trip, and I drew a diagram of a canvas seat that he was to make for me, one that could be suspended from poles and carried by coolies or rolled into a compact and lightweight package

unless I needed to ride in it to get to Leh. I called
it the Ambulance. I was determined that nothing
short of Time stopping altogether for me would
prevent my getting there. For the outstretched
Hand of Circumstance bribed me with the promise
of a world stretching like the fourth dimension
beyond the realm of experience; a promise that
outweighed fear and bodily handicaps. Not since
the days of 1915-16 when the "garde-à-vous" resounded through the night and "pompiers" dashed
through Paris' streets heralding a Zeppelin raid
had I felt that surge of blood which rises so stub-
bornly to meet an emergency.

And there was the lure of the road: Wild, fantastic mountains with "lamaseries" perched on
dizzy cliffs, miles of prayer walls covered with
stones carved with the mantra of Tibet: *"Om mané
padme hum"* and "chortens" that held "potted
lamas" or patties made from the ashes of the dead.
And on the road would be women wearing head-
dresses called "peyrak" that were studded with
turquoise and they would perhaps stick out their
tongues in greeting and say "zhu-le" instead of
the "salaam" I had grown accustomed to. And
beyond Leh was Hemis where lived a "skushok"
or reincarnated lama, and in Hemis also were Devil
Dances; and of course I would go to Hemis if
ever I got to Leh. And I would go too across the

Khardong Pass, 18,142 feet high, go on the back of a yak.

And the road ran among cliffs of gorgeous colouring and through the deepest gorge in the whole world, where reality itself became illusion and the fabric of wild imaginings were the commonplaces of every day. And along the road for six months of the year the customs and habits of the middle ages mingled with those of the twentieth century. And over the road it was possible to go right away from everything that one had ever known, to where subways and radios and airplanes and ships and motors and trolley cars and electric lights and all such modern trappings were unthinkable.

I have among my treasures other precious "Passes," notably a "Laissez Passer" from Paris dated July 27th, 1915. And a "Sauf Conduit" through the devastated region from Vitry-le-François to Nancy where one could hear the great guns booming at the front. Rare and difficult permits to obtain in those early war days. But the permit to travel to Ladakh under certain specified rules and conditions laid down in the enclosed Res Rules held no less interest when it arrived in the form of several long important-looking sheets.

These gave the revised rates of pony and coolie hire on the Treaty High Road, and the cost of putting up at the dak bungalows along the road.

Warnings and rules governing the crossing of frontiers and the sale of ammunition or arms were listed and the amounts of grain that might be taken from granaries along the route.

It was explained that Res Rules was a system by which a village or group of villages is bound to supply transport for certain stages of certain roads. It makes travel in those parts possible and is one of the reasons for the stringent limitation of passes and also accounts for the sad little objects that carry the heavy loads so patiently back and forth along those dangerous paths in all kinds of weather, and who, at the end of a march, stand with drooping heads and sagging muscles, and often with sore eyes that run with pus. On almost every back are the white patches of hair that show where sores have been. For the way a sore is treated along the road is to cover it with a piece of cloth and apply a match to it. The resulting ashes are supposed to form a coating which heals the wound more quickly and fits the back to bear once more its burden! A chapter might be written about those poor little animals, the tragedy of the road. Fed, or rather underfed, for the most part on what grass they can find on the hills surrounding the compound, they are turned loose to graze each night and are recaptured at dawn. Heaven knows when they get sleep.

I had had the men instructed at the start to accept no ponies with sore backs, but the enforcement of this rule was not always possible, for new ponies were brought in before dawn, saddled and packed in the dark, and the caravan was well on its way before its infringement could be noted.

Once after riding through miles of the desert on a wretched horse that was weak in its hind legs I started to change my saddle to the back of the one ridden by my bearer and found that his saddle had covered a raw spot on the pony's side as large as my hand. Needless to say I continued on my own mount and had the other poor beast led for the rest of the way, but little comforted by the thought of his respite, for the return journey, usually undertaken after a brief rest, would surely be under the weight of his master or of another load.

At last the day came when I set out on the road which is actually the Golden Road to Samarkand if you will turn north beyond Leh over the dread Khardong Pass and follow over the worse Saser Pass into Chinese Turkestan. As final preparation I staged a bit of illness, the kind doctor saying: "Is there anyone in authority over you who can prevent your making this trip? Why can't you be content with going to Sonamarg and camping there?"

"Why should I stay in Sonamarg when I can go to Leh?"

"With a pulse like that you have no business to go!" was the reply.

I made laughing rejoinder: "Dear Doctor, life was meant for experience."

So often in the past I had been confronted with risks that promised fuller living. Friends or doctors had tried to hitch me to safety posts with good advice. In every instance adventuring had made life richer. Sometimes I had paid dearly for experience. . . . It was worth the price.

And here once more such a decision to make!

What made me go?

It has been said that women have a better time in life than men because more things are forbidden them. Yet it was not perversity that urged me on. I reviewed the horrors of the trip. . . . I was scared to death.

But it meant absorbing more of the world's magic. Not to go would be limiting life . . . too high a price to pay for the back yard of safety!

Beyond was a new world . . . and tense, swift living. I had always loved that poem by John Neihardt:

Let me live out my years in heat of blood!
Let me die drunken with the dreamer's wine!

Let me not see this soul-house made of mud
Go toppling to the dusk—a vacant shrine.

Let me go quickly, like a candle light
Snuffed out just at the heyday of its glow.
Give me high noon—then let it be night!
Thus would I go.

And grant that when I face the grisly thing
My soul may trumpet down the gray Perhaps,
Let me be as a tune-swept fiddle string
That feels the Master Melody—and snaps!

What more could one hope from life than that the song should cease on a high note? What more could one ask of death than that it should come as one climbed to new heights?

A friend I value once quoted to me a saying of E. S. Martin:

"The fortunate people, the truly fortunate, are not so much those who succeed in life as those who succeed in living."

Of course I would go to Leh!

And so a week later I returned to Srinagar from the higher hills of Gulmarg to prepare for the great day.

CHAPTER III

Mrs. Duncan, Mr. Phelps and I had arranged to meet on July fifteenth at Nedou's Hotel in Srinagar.

I being the first one to arrive engaged three adjoining rooms.   Mrs. Duncan greeted me at tiffin and we decided to spend the afternoon resting.   There would be enough work for the three of us to do next day.

Mr. Phelps bustled in at tea time. Through the Venetian blinds across my window I saw his bearer sorting his effects out on the wide veranda that ran across the house.   I had left a note for him saying:

"We will meet at cocktail time . . . eight o'clock . . . in the main building.   I have reserved a table for dinner."

We met as arranged.

Much wit passed around with the cocktails . . . mostly at my expense as I sketched a mental picture of my gargoyle costume and of my worse than ignorant actions on a horse.

43

We dined . . . about nineish, as the English say. We had a table to ourselves.

I presented my problems: Word had come to me that the shikari-cook that I had been keeping on all summer for the trip was not to be trusted. He was said to have paid five rupees to a coolie to shove a man over the cliff on one of his trips. The men he had chosen were all of his family. He controlled the bandobast. More than one person had warned me not to take him with me. "He plans trouble," they told me. I recalled that he had been disgruntled when he heard that Mr. Phelps would bring his personal servant with him. He had opposed it. And he had shown anger when I announced that another woman and her servant would join the bandobast. We would have to take considerable money with us to last for the trip. This would be at his mercy along the road where it must be carried with our equipment. To change the outfit would mean delay . . . What should I do?

"My man is handy about camp and most willing, but he is a Gurkha and will not wait at table," Mrs. Duncan said.

"My 'bearer' is new . . . a Kashmiri. He avoids work as if it were an indelicacy. But he speaks English." This was my contribution.

"Better make a clean sweep of the snakes," said

Mr. Phelps. "My boy has been with me for years. He's invaluable. I'll help you to select a new outfit. Let's fire them to-night!"

"No, I have a better plan," I said. "We'll get the stores and equipment packed into the lorries to-morrow and put your man to guard them. Then I'll fire the whole bunch." And so it happened.

An Agency sent us several men to select from. None of them spoke English, so Mr. Phelps questioned them in Urdu, showed me their chits, and together we selected the outfit.

First Kadera, cook-guide, tall, lean and strong, with the look of a hawk in his eyes that met ours unflinchingly. His chits stated that in all of the Passes of Kashmir he was at home, and that the Burzil Choka that led across the lonely wastes of the Deo Sai plains were as familiar to him as were the tracts across Bot Kol glacier and the Kolahoi. As we planned to make the return journey by one of these equally alluring routes I was glad to be able to depend on this man whose eyes, furrowed about by rain and sun and wind—and years, looked out so fearlessly. On the road Kadera often fell into step beside my pony or trailed with me as I pulled my rebellious feet over stony ground, and I wanted much to talk to him of the wide horizons he had seen. But all that he could express was

his willingness to serve and what he understood
from me was only my love of his hills and The
Road.

The "bishti's" name was so similar to Kadera's
that I dubbed him "Happy" because he always
smiled and in so doing showed a row of beautiful
teeth; his chit was brief. He had only one and it
was none too enthusiastic. But I liked him and
when, waving his long awkward arms, he assured
us that he could do just anything, we took him
on. And it was Happy who trudged beside me
along the road carrying my water bottle and
moving picture camera and who held my stirrup
when I mounted and who did everything he was
told to do most willingly—unless he forgot. After
I found out that he could not carry a thought long
under the skull cap that was disguised by the dirt
of ages, it was simple to remind him frequently.
It was Happy who saw the dawns with me from
mountain peaks and who was usually far away
when I needed my camera most.

Then there was the sweeper who would do little
in camp because of the ostracism of his caste, and
who would sleep, I was advised not to ask where,
but not in the tents with the other servants. Thus
with our three bearers and these new men six personal servants accompanied us and were packed
into the two lorries with the equipment and stores.

Mr. Phelps went out with them to have the first camp ready by the time the two mem-sahibs motored out, which was to be at six in the evening.

Ganderbal is only thirteen and a half miles from Srinagar.

The ride out was over a good road which ran between rice fields with lovely mountain views all about. We found our first camp pitched beside the low banks of a river. There under the willow trees was our dining table already set. The camp fires were burning lustily.

We were in a delicious mood. Mr. Phelps suggested that we would get on much better if we called each other by our Christian names. He was nicknamed Sandy he said and we might use it or anything else that belonged to him.

"Call me Margot," said Mrs. Duncan.

Why do we not have Margots, Daphnes, Patricias, Jennifers and Phyllis's in America I wonder!

"And what would you call me?" I asked them. "My own name is long and formal."

"Let's call her the Duchess," suggested Mrs. Duncan.

"You're thinking of the one in Alice in Wonderland," I remarked. "You'll think it appropriate when you see me in my trekking costume."

"Burra mem-sahib is too formal for you also," said Sandy.

"What's a burra mem-sahib?" I asked.

"Burra means big, or important," explained Mr. Phelps. "This is your bandobast so of course you're the most important one and will be called that by the servants and will be served first at table."

"Too much 'izzat' for the road," I exclaimed.

They shortened my name to Rita.

Dinner was soon served out under the willows on the river's brink. The stars were our table lights. The swish of waters our orchestra. Just there at the bend the river was parted by great boulders over which the spray was driven high. Across on the other side stretched fields of ripening corn, while hugging the banks were several houseboats moored with their cookboats beside them. In the deepening dusk their lights cast long reflections over the water and from them came the chatter of natives and the crackle of kitchen fires.

Another scene leaped to memory:

And what a difference!

Then . . . a table laden with silver and flowers was set in a formal garden. The waters of Lake Constance lapped at the sea wall near by. Lackeys in red coats trimmed with gold lace waited behind each chair. Guests in evening attire sparkled with jewels.

All that the world endows of pomp and circumstance and worldly power glittered then under the
stars of Austria.

And now . . . the least of everything that comfort spells . . . and before us a long hard road.

The lights of the houseboats were extinguished
one by one. . . . Our voices trailed off into the
dusk.

There was greater enchantment at Ganderbal.

Our tents were an education in luxury. I had
had them set up by the roadside in Srinagar for
my inspection, but they better-bettered my first im-
pression of them.

They were lined with bright yellow cloth and
running down each side were gaily stenciled pockets fringed with red, blue and green. The tent
fly, blue-lined, formed a circular wash room at the
back and in front spread out umbrella-like to
shield from sun and rain. I had had gunny sewed
all around the bottom of the tents and this, held
down by the yakdans on one side and by cots on
the other, prevented wind and rain from driving
in. Waterproof canvas sheets covered the grass
floor, and these along the march served to protect
our bedding rolls.

My canvas bedding roll held extra sheets and
towels and all of the odds and ends that escaped
the yakdans. I had a lantern and a flashlight, a

clock-watch, a basin in leather cover, and a canvas toilet case that hung with my clothes from tent hooks on the rear tent pole. A folding canvas chair added the final touch to comfort.

The servants' tents called "pals" were pitched at some distance from our own and the ground about was strewn with camp equipment. There was the meat safe, a square wire-net box on wooden frame, where all perishable supplies were kept, and which was strapped to the back of a coolie who walked with it the whole distance between stages. For stove we had a sheet of iron with two large perforations in it. This was placed over a hole in the ground and supported by stones which were always to be found nearby. We bought enough twigs and branches at Ganderbal to take along for the next two stages.

We carried our canned and bottled goods in fourteen wooden boxes with hinged and padlocked lids and these were loaded two or more on each pony along with other equipment to balance. In order to save our supplies so as not to run short on the return journey we bought milk and eggs and some chickens at Ganderbal and at the few other places along the route where they were obtainable. We had started with a supply of fresh vegetables enough to last for the first two or three stages, and I had arranged with Nedou's Hotel

THE MEAT SAFE, A SQUARE WIRE NET BOX ON WOODEN FRAME, WHICH WAS STRAPPED
TO THE BACK OF A COOLIE.

I WONDERED WHAT IN THE WORLD KADERA WOULD DO IF HE WERE EVER OBLIGED
TO CONFINE HIMSELF TO THE LIMITS OF A KITCHEN IN A FLAT.

THEN THE PONIES CAME IN.

in Srinagar to ship up canned butter to various
stages along the road. It always came on time
and kept fresh throughout the whole trip, being
put in a bag that was tethered to the river bank
and left floating in the water at night to keep it
cool. No ice can be purchased in Kashmir or along
the road, though sometimes in Kashmir snow is
brought down from the mountains in sacks for
freezing purposes.

We decided to hold over a day at Ganderbal
where there was post and telegraph office in case
we found something lacking in supplies, and to
enable our hastily assembled staff to become
acquainted with one another and the equipment.
Also we felt the need of a day's rest after the hectic
time we had had in Srinagar.

At Ganderbal we engaged twenty-two pack
ponies and three saddle horses which were to stay
with us all the way to Dras, the first eighty-nine
miles of the journey. We were lucky for it is not
always possible to secure Dras pony men at Ganderbal, and they are preferable to Kashmiris, the
latter being notorious for thievery and cowardice.

Again the horse chosen for me was called Lalla.
I rode him for a bit, or rather I got on him and
turned him round twice the night before starting,
hoping that he was as good as they said he was.

As much of the kit as could be sorted was stacked the night before our start ready for loading at dawn, and I fell asleep to the tune of swishing waters and a light patter of rain on the canvas above me.

CHAPTER IV

TREKKING—THE FIRST FIVE STAGES

I RUBBED sleepy eyes next morning when the camp alarm clock sounded at three. Peering out I saw figures creeping about with swinging lanterns by whose glimmer the servants' pals were being struck and kit packed for the march, no easy job in the dark, by lantern light; and had not every article of clothing been conveniently laid out before retiring, dressing by candlelight would also have been difficult. But it was swift work and I was lacing my boots when my bearer came with "chota hazri," that inevitable eye-opener in India which is coffee and rolls in some places, and "petit déjeuner" in others and here just a cup of hot tea and some biscuits to warm one before the early and cold start.

All of the pony men were lending aid, and as soon as each tent was vacated it was struck and rolled and placed along with the kit that was to go on the same pony, each piece securely fastened on to gunny strips. Ponies were then led up to the piles, the gunnies were lifted up and dropped

53

across long padded Kashmiri saddles and tightly strapped to the ponies who stood patiently waiting to be driven on to the road.

Dawn was just breaking as we started. I, on my strange Lalla, was grateful that the road was to lie flat and uneventful for some miles until I felt more confidence. By design, I think, the first stages are made as short as they are easy, and each stage a little more difficult to accustom one by degrees to the hardships of the road.

From Ganderbal a broad, flat motor road runs for five miles as far as Weyil Bridge which is suspended across the Sind River. We passed villages and for much of the way the road ran under spreading branches. Beyond the bridge it became monotonous winding beside the river, a road hot under the later sun but traversed by us in the cool of early morning. We made the whole of the stage in six and a half hours, only to find that the dak bungalow at Kangan, the largest and best on the road, was full. We went on a couple of miles beyond, crossed a stream and a rock-strewn field and pitched our tents near a grove of willows by the river bank, here even lower than at Ganderbal, and with a bridge close by made of two logs without railings. The water rushed loudly past, pine-covered mountains rose on all sides with sacred Haramok at 16,872 feet closing the valley's end. Dark, gaunt, forbidding crags rode the air like an embattled grey castle among the verdant hills. Behind it lay Gangabal Lake, where at an elevation of twelve thousand feet is supposed to be the source of the sacred River Ganges.

It was interesting to watch the caravan come in. First the meat-safe coolie arrived, sat himself on the ground and slid out of the rope harness that attached to his back. The "stove," one piece of perforated sheet iron, was soon in action. There were so many holes already among the rocks that it wasn't long before it was set up, covered with our cook pots and water cans and a lusty fire going under it.

Then the ponies came in.

Hill ponies, appropriately called "tats," are tiny things with hoofs so small that their shoes, when they are shod at all, are hardly larger than a good-sized brooch. Though burdened with nearly two hundred pounds of equipment, with bulky tents and bedding rolls, unwieldly tent poles, boxes, baskets, chairs, pots and pans, they trudge along one close behind the other, heads down . . . but never flagging.

Along with each pony walks a pony man, usually the owner, whose duty it is to keep him to the path, to watch for oncoming caravans and help his charge past them on narrow ledges. For loaded ponies to try to pass each other without this assistance would probably end in disaster.

Scattered among our pack ponies were coolies who carried such things as lanterns and oil tins which could not well be packed on a jolting pony. Our own men were distributed among the outfit to maintain order and control. It made a splendid moving picture. As soon as the caravan was in, the pony men unstrapped the loads and lifted the gunny strips with their contents and the ponies walked out from under.

While the bearers pitched our tents, set up the cots and chairs and distributed each one's effects in the proper tents Kadera was busy strewing the ground with his kitchen paraphernalia. I wondered what in the world he would do if he were ever condemned to confine himself to the limits of a kitchen in a flat. His effects must have covered an acre of ground; pots, pans, boxes and baskets of food spread everywhere, and the cook tent handy by the meat safe.

Someone had brought a "hookah," that peace pipe of the East, and every now and then one of the men would stop work long enough to dash over to where it stood and take a few puffs to fortify himself. Everyone was busy, and all talked at once, and everything seemed to be accomplished at once, for in no time at all we were made comfortable, had hot water for our baths, and a good meal. The ponies meanwhile had wandered down to the river or were resting in the shade of the willow grove near by. It rained fitfully during the afternoon, rendering canvas heavier and more difficult to handle for the morrow. . . .

For those who have ready access to open spaces, who can go off "into the blue" whenever they desire, I suppose there cannot be the grip of such enchantment as fills the city dweller freed for a brief space amidst "the solemn hush of dreaming solitudes." A ringed moon in a clearing sky, the smell of wet earth and of thick pine forests come to one as a great experience; the silence itself a wonder to ears that even in sleep have registered the vibration of subway trains, the horns of motors and the clang of elevated cars. The patter of rain on the canvas was a soothing sound; it was so dry and cosy in the tents.

We left Kangan the next day far too late for the fourteen mile trek to Gund. We did not start until six-thirty, two hours after dawn and the heat was intense that July day. My cork spine pad and Mespot topi with its circular shield did duty through the seven hours that it took us to reach Gund, hours made doubly uncomfortable by swarms of tiny flies that pestered the ponies also. . . .

Beyond Kangan the road grew lovelier, some-

times mounting along embankments or rock cutting high above the Sind River which was churned
and lashed into rapids or fed by icy waterfalls
from high peaks that brought a welcome coolness
to the lower levels. The road rose and fell, sometimes crossing the river over narrow plank bridges
guiltless of rails or fording the foaming waters
that cast their spray over us. Then higher and
higher it wound, leaving the Sind far below.

Fields of rice and corn were gay with wild
flowers. Yellow asters, Siberian wall flowers of
yellow and orange, columbine and wild geranium
were everywhere. Lazy cattle refused to yield us
the road. They knew that their sacred persons
were safe from molestation.

A few villages were passed. Family groups
squatted under the wide branches of "chenar." We
saw Kashmiri women, their great earrings swinging as they moved, their dark trousers striped with
many colours, anklets and bracelets jingling. In
Srinagar one sees them only in the time-honoured
long robe of dusky red, the costume of both men
and women.

The road to Gund is a gradual ascent. Gund itself lies at six thousand five hundred feet.

I trailed into camp weary and hot to find Margot and Sandy loafing under the spreading
branches of a huge walnut tree, sipping their

whiskies and sodas as nonchalantly as if they had been on the veranda of the club at Srinagar.

Margot had lived years in India and was hardened to trekking among the mountains. She was also used to heat and glare. She preferred to walk, and Sandy seemed to feel that he had to because a woman did. This usually brought them into camp ahead of me.

My feet, accustomed to asphalt pavements, could not negotiate more than a mile or so at a time over the stony, uneven paths. On horseback I could travel only at the pack pony's gait of two and a half miles an hour which is as fast as its short legs wlil take it at a walk. That was my pony's choice . . . and mine.

Sometimes I urged Lalla to a faster gait when a level bit of road appeared. But I was unable to learn the trick of rising in the stirrup and took and gave so much punishment in the bumps that I decided, with Lalla, that a walk was best.

Our men were busy pitching the tents on the edge of a high bluff below which the Sind River struggled and protested loudly against its confinement between narrow banks. It was cool under the trees. A breeze wafted down the sweet scent of pines.

Margot and Sandy were gay. I caught their mood tired as I was.

"But why the tents . . . with a perfectly good and empty dak bungalow close at hand?" I questioned.

"It's occupied already," Margot replied.

"I don't see a soul about," I declared.

"It's fuller than the one at Kangan was. In fact it's overcrowded," Sandy explained.

"Natives?" I asked.

"Yes. It seems that they live here all the year round," said Sandy. "By virtue of squatter's rights they eject anyone who tries to put up at the bungalow."

"That's funny! I thought it was a rule of the road that one could not remain over twenty-four hours if a newcomer needed the room."

"They have the most convincing argument," said Margot. Then Sandy quoted:

"Great fleas have little fleas upon their backs to bite 'em,
And little fleas have lesser fleas, and so ad infinitum.
And the great fleas themselves, in turn, have greater
    fleas to go on,
While these again have greater still, and greater still,
    and so on."

"Well, the limit has at last been reached," exclaimed Margot. "I read in the papers some time ago that the smallest flea has actually been found by experts from the London School of Hygiene and Tropical Medicine."

"Bet they had camped at Gund!" exclaimed Sandy.

We sprayed the ground under and around our tents with Flit and pitied the poor ponies who at Gund are not driven up into the hills to graze on account of poisonous grass there, but are tethered in front of the serai and fed lucerne which we had brought from Ganderbal for them.

The mess tent was a convenience at Gund . . . a luxury, but not a necessity. We had a delicious luncheon served there. Chicken, fresh vegetables, scones, butter and jam. Sandy was pensive.

"A penny, Sandy . . ." I began the trite phrase. He interrupted . . .

"No wonder that the House of Commons once solemnly debated the question of whether fleas are animals or insects to determine their classification under the bill to regulate the treatment of stage animals. They could jump thirty times their own height and pull eight times their own weight, it was argued, and they were the most wonderful workers in the whole world . . . independent of Labour Unions."

"Yet we in America assert that the English have no sense of humour!" I ejaculated.

My bearer Abdullah was a Kashmiri. Having noted that Margot's Gurkha did not wait at table he decided that he would forego the pleasure also.

Sandy, our housekeeper, thought differently. A few words escaped Abdullah. Sandy boxed his ears. Discipline had to be maintained so the Burra mem-sahib got into action. Result: Abdullah, one pony, bedding roll and pay to date started back towards Kashmir. This left me without a personal servant and Sandy's Ali, who was already doing the work of two, added me to his cares.

We were sitting under the trees after dinner. It was silent but for the crackling of the campfire and the roar of the river. Then old Kadera came up to us. His eyes had a feverish glitter and he spoke in whispers:

"They sometimes come in bands at night . . . the Afridis. They come down over the hills and loot the caravans. Keep an eye out, sahib . . . they have been known to carry men off from here."

He spoke in Hindustani. Sandy translated.

"Pipe dreams!" he explained.

He talked to Kadera as one might converse with a child. He let him have his say and assured him that we would be vigilant.

"The old fellow's lonely," he said to us when Kadera retired to the campfire where the other

THE ROCK LEDGE OF THE ZOJI-LÀ.

AT TEN THOUSAND FEET OUR CAMP WAS PITCHED.

FOR MOST OF THE WAY IT WAS A HARD UP HILL PULL FOR PACK PONIES.

men were huddled. "I think that he's a hemp smoker. They act like that."

It was clear and cool when we left next morning at six o'clock for the rougher road that runs up and down beside the widening river and is famous for its beauty. The country was ever more fertile, ever more thickly strewn with flowers. We turned in through shady groves, the ponies treading carefully over partly sunken tree roots. The country-side flaunted its flowers more recklessly.

Then a long gorge—Gagangir—shut us in and the road became a mere track between stupendous cliffs so close and so high that we saw their tips only with craning necks. Higher and higher climbed the road, up rock ladders and down shale slopes and on again through fragrant pine forests; then out again where vistas of glaciers spread before us and clouds floated like veils of gossamer across dark mountain sides.

Lalla, calm and sure-footed, carried me up the rock ladders and down steep slopes with never a stumble, stopping to get his breath when a steep pull proved too long and walking on without coaxing when he felt able to once more. He crossed and recrossed high narrow bridges of flimsy planks which gave me the sensation of being perched in the air between sky and water, but he was so gentle that I was unafraid and glad that the rules of the road permitted me to carry him and all of the ponies across the dreaded Zoji-Là and into Dras. On Lalla's back I soon felt so safe that I could enjoy the scenery without constantly being on the alert for mishaps. And there was so much of beauty to see. Jets of water springing out from high cliffs. Vistas of snow peaks between green hills, and the winding rushing river. Suddenly I urged Lalla past a dreadful spot where lay the rotting carcass of a pony that had fallen off the embankment. Along the road, the poor beast that slips from the path finds no burial and eventually its bones are used to bolster the fences by the wayside. Zos, these a cross between yak and cow, laden with great bundles of rugs from Yarkand passed us on the last lap of their long journey into Kashmir and for the first time we heard the Tibetan greeting "zhu-le," instead of the familiar "salaam" . . .

The valley widened and there spread range on range of grey and green mountains holding imperishable snows between their ridges, their bases resting in wide fields of wild flowers. Acres and acres of forget-me-nots, looking like frost on the slopes, were relieved here and there by patches of mustard. Wild flowers were everywhere—a riot of colour, tall yellow and orange Siberian wall flowers, larkspur, monkshood, blue gentian, spiræa, meadowsweet, pink hawthorn and wild geranium. The river wound white and unruffled here just below the road, the air heavenly cool off the snows, and there, at ten thousand feet, our camp was pitched at convenient distance from the second post and telegraph office, the first since Ganderbal . . .

The trip from Gund to Sonamarg is fourteen and a half miles, and for most of the way is a hard up-hill pull for pack ponies and ours did not come in until long after we did. We lay under a tree resting in a field of wild flowers until they arrived and tents were pitched. The first thought then as always was of the bath, and Happy and the coolies filled the petrol tins from the river. As we went higher the water took longer to boil. At sea level it boils at 212,° but it cannot be brought to heat above 180° at an altitude of ten thousand feet, and it also took our food longer to cook. We had had breakfast along the road, somewhere about eight thirty, for the tiffin coolie with tiffin basket and thermos bottles strapped to his back always followed at a convenient distance.

Because the day's march had been strenuous, and because such beauty called for more than the worship of one night, we decided to linger next day amid that loveliness where cool breezes fanned us and veils of mist hid and then revealed strange

mountain peaks and glaciers lay like crumpled silk
between tall pines. Years ago Sonamarg, which
means "Meadows of Gold," was the chief sanitar-
ium of Kashmir, but was later abandoned for Gulmarg the more accessible. Yet always camping
parties have sought its wide "margs" and "nul-
lahs" from which many paths lead off to the adventures of Thajwas, Kolahoi and Amarnath.

It was good to unpack and look forward to a
long rest next morning. There was much sorting
of one's baggage to be done in camp, and clothes
to be washed out and dried on the tent ropes.
There were also my films to be wrapped carefully
in the oil cloth I had brought along for the purpose. On top of that I put waterproof paper for
they had a long journey to make down to Bombay to be processed. Taken in ever increasing altitude, both in cold and burning heat and glare,
and dampness, they had to be carried along to the
next stage that boasted a postoffice from whence
they journeyed back over the road to Ganderbal.
Sometimes parcel mail waits at a postoffice along
the road until a whole pony load is collected so
there is delay everywhere. It has all to be sorted
after arriving at Ganderbal where it is put on a
lorry for Srinagar and from there transferred to
another lorry for the trip across the mountains
to the railroad station at Rawal Pindi down in In-

dia; from Pindi it goes by train to Bombay, and there, at sea level, the films are processed on Monday only of every week. In spite of all this I have a fairly good record of the trip, though never of the worst bits of the road of rock ledges or of the fordings when I merely hoped to get by and never thought of taking pictures.

Along the road we travelled as in a "Caucus-Race," each one taking his own gait more or less together over the very bad places, then each one straggling into camp as best suited his taste or his strength. But a day in camp throws you with your fellow travellers more intimately.

Certainly one of the most interesting things about knocking around the world is acquaintance with the many different types of people you meet. Sometimes they have your pass word—often they have not. Sometimes they brush you with their wings and remain in your consciousness for ever. Sometimes their eyes register unfinished dreams and set you to wondering. Sometimes their humour gilds the hours with laughter. And sometimes they tempt you to paraphrase old Samuel Butler:

> We grant, although they had much wit
> They were very shy of using it;
> As being loath to wear it out
> And therefore bore it not about,

Unless on holidays or so,
As men their best apparel do.

Sandy had withstood the first shock of my appearance gallantly. But forewarned is not always forearmed and my looks were about as popular with him as a promissory note. He liked to stride ahead of me and he always gave me plenty of time to change to more attractive raiment before he sought my society in camp.

And how interesting, the sounds of camp! The crackling fire; the smell of cooking; the rattle of equipment; the restlessness of horses tethered near or roaming wild; the animated voices of thirty men all talking at one time, the pony men withdrawn a distance from the camp, our own attendants gathered about the fire busily engaged in preparing comforts for us. They are tireless, these natives; after a long day's march they uncomplainingly care for the sahib's needs, polishing his boots, washing out his clothes, and even ironing them with red hot embers in an empty tin cracker box, or as the English call it, "biscuit box." You do not scold if your most cherished shirtwaist is badly burned —the intent was good. You do not argue if, the water tasting better than usual, you shower compliments and receive the answer: "Sometimes the pot is clean, Hazoor." Out come the "hookahs" after evening meal. The prayers of prostrate men upwing—a thing so beautiful in the East in its simple unconscious reverence that takes no thought of surroundings. . . .

The day under a burning sun was over, its glare softened into shadows along the soaring peaks; blankets of forget-me-nots trailed their beauty along the fringe of such austerity like flowers held between the fingers of the dead. Everywhere forget-me-nots.

And looking over acres and acres of wildflowers I thought: "Should one not grant to their beauty the germ of immortality as Buddhists do? Are they not of the immeasurable things?" . . .

I awoke next day to see the stretch of meadow in front of my tent flooded with sunshine. It was not late but I heard muffled voices from the mess tent. Margot and Sandy breakfasting together. In good old Indian style I raised my voice and cried lustily:

"Quai Hai."

The Burra mem-sahib had spoken!

Ali appeared in a flash. Ali was always in khaki: baggy trousers; shirt hanging over them; coat of any sort; turban with long end hanging down his back. He invariably had a duster slung over his arm or across his shoulder. Ali without his duster would have been Ali only partly dressed.

I suspected that he dusted the table, the plates and the equipment impartially with it. Behind Ali came Margot and Sandy.

"How is the Burra mem-sahib?" asked Margot.

"I'll race you to the postoffice," I cried gleefully. "I feel twenty years younger. What glorious air!"

"You'll do no racing in this sun or altitude," asserted Margot.

Noticing her costume which consisted of a short-sleeved shirtwaist and pair of shorts I remarked with a wise smile:

"Going fishing?"

Her eyes twinkled as she put her arm through Sandy's and replied: "Only for snow trout . . . cold little things. Are you joining us?"

"Don't ask me to plan a day before I've had breakfast. What's in the larder, Sandy?"

"Oatmeal. Eggs. Bacon. Scones and butter. Tea or coffee as you prefer."

"It's not enough," I exclaimed. "I could eat the whole of a sacred cow."

"Give her sausages, Sandy, you've been hoarding them."

"We'll starve on the way home if we feed her like this every day. We can't get supplies in Leh and we're not half there yet."

"While you two argue the point of whether I'm

to be starved now, tell Ali to rustle the tea and oat-meal. And while he's doing it both of you sit here and amuse me." This they did.

"I feel strong enough now to pack up my films," I declared after I'd eaten enough for two meals at home. "Will you mail them for me Sandy?"

"No," he replied. "I'll *post* them."

We had fun emphasizing the differences between English and American. They spoke of flats . . . I called them apartments. Candy was sweets to them; their elevators were lifts. They said topping while I cried bully. They spoke of a proper saddle that was a good one to me. Cupboards to them were closets to me. I learned that an English girl never had a beau . . . merely a "young man"; and that not one "cunning" baby exists in the realm.

When I asked Sandy for crackers he questioned:

"What are they? They sound noisy like the fourth of July." What I described he said were "biscuits."

"We make those fresh every day," I exclaimed disdainfully.

"You print on your packages 'Uneeda Biscuit,' " he retorted. I was crushed, but rallied.

"Why should you expect that Americans would talk like you? You don't talk like yourselves." America's flag was still flying.

Margot and Sandy went fishing while I got dressed.

Sandy's whistle . . . all out of tune, floated up to me from where they were coaxing reluctant trout.

Funny world! Here I was . . . far away from civilization . . . in the heart of the Himalayas, with people I'd never laid eyes on a short while ago.

It reminded me of an experience that I had had in France during the war. Then also in a silent, lonely place with a man and a woman companion . . . known even less than I knew these two. There was devastation all about us . . . we picked up broken spoons, obus, and torn pages of prayer books in German from the trenches.

I had been lucky to get the difficult permit to leave Paris, a safe conduct through to Vitry-le-François, and a permit to journey on beyond.

"We can give you no information about conditions beyond Vitry," said the Secretary of War to me. "The lines are down . . . all communication is cut off. It is devastated region. I've no idea whether you will find a place to sleep or not."

The American Ambassador had helped me to get the permit.

I was dining at the Embassy two nights before I was to start, and there I met a little French-woman who was all eagerness to accompany me.

"Be at the France et Choiseul at eight-thirty day after to-morrow," I said. "And if the Secretary of War will permit you to go with me I'd be delighted to have you."

And the night before my departure, I was dining in the hotel. Someone had come up and greeted a man who sat at the table just behind me. I recognized the name of Dr. K—— whom a friend had several times asked to meet me. We had never been able to dine or lunch with her at the same time.

"Speak to him if you see him in the hotel," she said to me. After his visitor had left I did so. He joined me and politely wished that he might see something of me during the rest of my stay in Paris. I told him that I was going up through the devastated regions back of the front the next day.

"How in the world did you manage it?" he exclaimed. "I've been here for months and have pulled every wire to get a permit and haven't been able to."

"Things always seem to come my way," I answered. "A cabinet officer suggested it and our Ambassador seconded the motion."

"You're in luck . . . wish I was going!"

"Be ready at eight-thirty to-morrow morning and go with me to the War Department. I have to get my final papers. If they will let you go along I'd love it. I've an idea that we could use a man on that trip."

"We?"

"I told him about the Frenchwoman and advised him as I had advised her to take only the absolute necessities which could all go in my one small bag. This we could carry in turn.

I was required to vouch for them and we started out within the hour. We had everything to learn about each other except our names . . . and had a wonderful adventure together. I've never seen or heard of either of them since.

And after this adventure we likewise would separate. Our paths lay oceans apart.

Margot was intangible. She was like a carefree boy at times as she strode along the road, and yet everything that was feminine, even to her rouge and lip stick, when she appeared for dinner in camp.

Sandy was as definite as an English lawn stretching peacefully across the acres . . . a perfectly well regulated young man whose crop of wild oats had never been Jimson weeds.

Life for me had been like a shorthand lesson. Vivid impressions . . . often changing scenes. Home address spread across continents and oceans. There had been victory and defeat, limelight and oblivion, plenty and poverty . . . life had often overcharged me. Much that I had tried to build had warped . . . and let in light.

By the time that I had bathed and dressed Margot and Sandy had returned. A string of trout was held up for my admiration.

"Let's climb to the glacier," I exclaimed. It hung on the slopes above us.

"Aren't we comfortable here? Let's loaf, and chat and quarrel . . . and sleep." Margot suggested.

"There's plenty of strenuous trekking ahead." Sandy settled the question.

We had each brought some books along. Propped against cushions we sat in a veritable flower garden. Margot and I read. Sandy stretched himself full length and whistled . . . still out of tune.

We were friendly, but impersonal . . . at least until the cow interfered.

One seems to have the whole world to oneself at Sonamarg. There are no habitations except by the postoffice, and this was not too near us. We felt safe from molestation and we no longer kept an eye on our effects. We hung our clothes on the ropes of our tents when we went to bed. The air was dry.

As usual we were astir early on the day that we

moved on to Baltal. We had settled into a routine. But this was now upset. Sandy was calling:

"Ali, where are my shorts?"

"What's the matter with him?" I asked Margot whose tent was close to mine. "He's been calling that for five minutes." Sandy had spoken in Urdu. Margot knew a few words of it.

"He's lost something," she explained.

"For heaven's sake, Sandy, what's missing? You haven't mislaid your original sin I hope," I called in to him.

There was a long silence while Ali and Sandy were heard moving about his tent and speaking now in low tones. Then Ali was heard departing.

"Something mysterious," I called to Margot. "Here, Sandy, is another flashlight."

"Don't come near me!" There was suffering in his tone.

"What in heaven's name" . . . began Margot, then we hushed and listened: Sandy was mumbling:

"They must be around here somewhere. I'm sure I hung them on the line last night."

"Sahib! Sahib!" Ali was seen approaching. His lantern revealed part of Sandy's grey woollen shorts which he held up in dismay. "The cow, sahib . . . the cow has eaten them!"

"Damn it . . . I've got to unpack that cursed yakdan and it's already strapped."

"Cheer up, Sandy. Here's something that will do until you get to Baltal." I threw over to him the short woollen skirt which I usually wrapped around outside my breeches for the cold morning start and had handy in my carryall. He fished it into his tent with a khud stick.

"If the cow doesn't mind we won't object," Margot called to him. But I noticed that this time Sandy walked behind me.

We took the road once more for Baltal just as dawn broke over the mountains colouring snow peaks and lighting up fields of gold and blue and the thousand-tinted blooms that flaunted their symphonies amidst bearded wheat. The air was cold, bracing and clean, and everything was crisp and green along our flower-strewn path.

There was one bad crossing of a river that rushed between banks so swiftly that it made foothold in the water difficult. The pack ponies were driven over with some misgivings while we clambered along the bank to a place where a tree had been thrown across. On this we stepped sideways making our way back to the road on the other side by holding on to branches and tree roots along the embankment. Sharp bends and narrow ribbon paths led on among cliffs where men and women from across far hills come to herd their flocks in Kashmir's fertile valley, Gujars these, lonely shepherds wrapped in drab blankets, their women with strange, wide, beautiful eyes outlined with kohl and hair wonderfully arranged in many braids drawn over a high frame, their necks and ankles and wrists strung with silver. Solemnly they greeted us: "Salaam, Hazoor!"

Some narrow swaying bridges were crossed, my Lalla never wavering as we mounted slopes and stepped over narrow planks, while far below the river dashed into high foam. I tried several of these crossings on foot and came to feel that Lalla negotiated them more steadily than I. And then we came to Baltal, at the foot of gigantic cliffs in a high birch glade nine miles from Sonamarg; a glade where more pink hawthorn and meadow sweet and balsam scented the air; where golden oreoles that Kashmiris call "Pashnool" flitted among the boughs; where cuckoos called; where there were sounds of waterfalls.

This was our first stop in a dak bungalow. The house was empty, and to make the early start next day, as one must to cross the Zoji-Là before the sun begins to melt the ice crusts, we unpacked as little as possible. Dak bungalows are usually built square with a porch across the front, and divided into four rooms, two bedrooms and two dressing rooms with bathroom alongside. One or two bungalows along this route have more accommodation but ordinarily they are for two people only. They all have high ceilings, white plastered walls, one or two windows and open fireplaces in each room, one or two chairs, tables, mirrors, and "charpoys" or, occasionally, iron beds. The floors are covered with rag rugs called "durries" in India, and pegs are driven into the walls to hang one's clothes on. The bathrooms, as everywhere in India, have sloping corners of cement with a hole to let water drain outside. Sometimes there is a basin, but always a round tin tub which one had best wash carefully with permanganate before using. Each dak bungalow is in charge of a "chowkidar" who presents his ledger at the end of your stay and you must write therein the hour of your arrival and of your departure and the amount of money you have paid to him.

At the rear of the bungalow is a "serai" for ponies and pony men; this is an open courtyard surrounded by small rooms, in which these men can sleep and cook. At Baltal the serai had been demolished by an avalanche a few weeks before we arrived; the same avalanche had sagged one corner of the bungalow. Our men pitched their "pals" near by. During the night the cook's blanket and part of the sweeper's shirt were devoured by a cow. We had already learned to put the more tempting delicacies of raw leather out of the way of pariah dogs that prowl about all night.

The dak bungalow at Baltal was clean, which means, not swept or dusted, but free from lice or other vermin, and we found it most liveable. No one minds dust along the road. If one can endure to have a choking cloud of it raised, the sweeper will brush off the durrie with his brush of twigs and lift all the dirt that has been trodden into the carpet by preceding travellers. I preferred not to raise a smoke screen but to add my quota to what former occupants had left and so cleared only enough space on table and chairs and charpoy to accommodate myself and my belongings. My clothes could not be harmed by any amount of dust as they were already specimens of hard wear. My face was blistered and my hair was like straw.

It did not matter; I was toughening up each day and ahead for the morrow lay the Zoji-Là; the long dreaded, much longed-for crossing of that first and worst pass, one of the five worst passes of all the Himalayan range. The Tibetans call it "Dud-ze-là," the "Four Devil Pass." It climbs two thousand feet up a sheer cliff in two miles, and runs for twenty miles into what Major Gompertz so truly calls "Magic Ladakh."

We were silent at dinner. Baltal is where one girds one's loins for the great event of the tomorrow. We had no illusions about the danger. The lower path across the snow beds of the Zoji-Là was impracticable at this season . . . the crusts might not hold. We should have to mount the path that leads steeply up, a narrow ledge carved along the mountain, curving in and out around its face, a sheer precipice at one side.

"You would be in an awkward position if anything happened to me," I finally exclaimed. "Let's be practical about it! *If* anything happens to me just dig me in by the road side and wire the American Consul in Calcutta. He has all further instructions. And don't turn back."

"The Residency, Srinagar, would be the place to send any notification about me," Margot stated. And Sandy said, "You already know my address."

We sought our cots soon after dinner. Sleep that night was a fitful thing for me.

Snow bridges and snow beds and rock ledges and rock ladders to cross! Could I make the grade, stand the altitude? Should I get sick and dizzy along the awful "khuds" and join my bones to the many that lay far down in the snows awaiting the trumpet call? The Zoji-Là! The Open Sesame to the loftiest inhabited district of the world! And mine the road that some of the greatest travellers

of the world had trod. At Baltal I never even
heard the crackling camp fires. I was listening
to other things; to the roar of imagined avalanches
and landslides; to the harrowing thud that said
"one more gone over," and then to the immense
silence.

CHAPTER V

ACROSS THE ZOJI-LÀ

"It's drizzling! Rotten weather!" Sandy's exclamation pierced the night.

"If it rains we had better wait over." This was by way of telling us that it was time to get up and start if we were to cross the dreaded pass.

Neve's words came back to me: "In wet weather the path is slippery, and a fall over the side is inevitably fatal."

And Sven Hedin had said, "The road up the Zoji-Là is along a wall of rock . . . steep, treacherous."

"We may be held up for days if a real storm breaks," Margot called from her room.

"The rain will soften the snow and make it all the worse to cross later if we wait," I volunteered.

"Well, hurry! Let's try it anyway!" Sandy spoke. "It's a tough pull along the rock ledge. We have to climb that before we reach the snow beds. We'll have to get across them before the sun comes up and melts the crust. It's soft at this season anyway."

83

"You're an optimist to be conjuring the sun on a day like this," I exclaimed. "It will be worse when the rain comes down, and I'm frozen already . . . two pairs of woollen stockings, fur-lined Gilgits and all."

"The dampness is penetrating! Keep your mufflers well up about your ears, girls."

Unnecessary advice.

"Don't forget your khud sticks . . . you'll need 'em!"

"How can I carry mine on horseback?" I cried.

"Give them to your pony boy!"

"All ready?"

"Let's start!"

"Let Happy go ahead of us with the lantern. I can't see a step ahead of me," called Margot.

"There, you fool, don't swing it out so that we're blinded by the light. Hold it in front of your body so that the light strikes the road and we can see where the damned thing is." That was Sandy speaking.

"How do you expect him to understand English? *Show* him!" said Margot.

Sandy grabbed the lantern and gave the necessary demonstration.

Happy walked on ahead . . . slowly. The ground was strewn with small sharp stones that had been hurled down by the avalanche. It was driz-

PURDAH WOMEN—HERE WAS THE SYSTEM IN FORCE EVEN ON THE LONELY ROAD
TO FAR LADAKH.

THE LOVELIEST DAK BUNGALOW OF THE WHOLE ROAD, . . .
AT SHIMSHI KHARBU,

THE SERAI WHERE OUR MEN WERE POLISHING BOOTS, ETC.

zling. What was not pitch black night was thick mist. Ye gods! To travel on a narrow, slippery, steep rock ledge in weather like this! My heart took up permanent abode on the end of my tongue.

Sandy followed Happy. I came next. Margot was behind me. It was bad going.

"We'll never get up to the top before dawn if we creep like this!" ejaculated Sandy.

"Before sunrise," I corrected wiping the mist off my face.

"Can't we make it a bit faster?"

"Set the pace. I'll keep it if I can but walking on eggs would be a cinch compared to this."

"Sandy still grumbling?" Margot called to me.

"A man's usual morning hate!" I called back to her.

At last. The up-grade began.

"Better get on your horse now," Sandy advised. "It will be stiff pulling." I mounted, whispered in Lalla's ear, and let him take his gait. I thanked my stars for Lalla, so surefooted was he, so careful in placing each little hoof on the slippery, rocky, narrow path. Often he had to step over boulders at up grade and again at down grade, with mist and rain obscuring and then revealing the path beyond and the sharp terrifying drop on the right.

I knew already by experience that it would be useless to urge him to leave the narrow track on the extreme edge made by countless tiny feet that had gone before—it would only distract and annoy him, and I did not dare. So with half of me hanging over that ghastly "khud" all the way up I had much the same sensation that I had had when on my first experience of flying we struck an air pocket while mounting two thousand feet in a tiny open Hispano-Suisa sea-plane. Only this time the sensation lasted longer. And if Adam had recorded the word "khud" in his famous diary he would have said that Eve named it that because she said that it looked like a "khud." And believe me it does! Not in the least like a precipice which word seems to allow the dignity of a slow descent. It is "khud"—brief and to the point, no mistaking it; the ragged edge of nothing.

Writers advise you to look between your horse's ears as you climb and try not to see the narrow ledge and not to think of the depths below. That English genius who claims to have discovered how to overcome the law of gravity might contemplate a fall over this khud without worry, but he would miss the real thrill of crossing the Zoji-Là. If you like diluted experiences by all means look between the pony's ears. But: "The cup of life's for him that drinks and not for him that sips." If you prefer the fullness of living you will look down the khud; look down to where between stark sheer

cliffs runs that pale ribbon of water winding its
way to the "Happy Valley"; look down and live
those moments out to their fullness or you will
never know what it really means to cross the Zoji-
Là. For it means the terror of danger; the thrill
of the unknown; all the Four Devils of the Pass
grimacing malevolently up at you while you feel
sick and wonder whether you're going to fall off
your horse down to where they seem to wait for
you.

But you don't fall; you'll suddenly acquire a
fierce knee grip, a sense of your own helplessness,
and when you try to describe your sensations thereafter you'll wonder at your inexpressiveness and
probably end up by saying with assumed bravery
as I did: "It wasn't as bad as I thought it was going to be."

But I had been conscious all the way of the hair's
breadth that divided me from the other world while
Lalla mounted on steady feet, with careful tread,
stopping every now and then to get his breath and
moving on to the cry of the pony man: "Kabardar!" "Kabardar!" "Take care!" "Take care!"

Many a time thereafter I called that word softly
into my pony's ear like a prayer when crossing narrow ledges or making bad fordings, and I cried it
out loud when an unexpected sharp drop over rocks
greeted me at a turn of the rocky ledge which was

too narrow to permit of dismounting. "Kabardar!"
"Kabardar!" And this alternated with "Ahista,"
pronounced asta, which does not mean haste as it
sounds, but is "slow" in Urdu.

Margot and Sandy were again on foot. I envied
them. They could pause and lean up against the
rocks that ran sheer up on the inner side. Sandy
ahead of me was getting his breath this way.

I wished that Lalla would move in away from
the edge over which one half of me hung. But
even when resting he held to the extreme outside.
I did not dare speak to him or to Sandy as I passed
him and now led the procession.

All this time we had been mounting the rock
ledge; it narrowed to a few inches over a sharp
drop. The path was almost wiped out by the remains of an avalanche that still clung in its ice
covering to the ledge over which it had swept weeks
before, carrying to their death twelve ponies and
four men whose remains even then were being dug
out of the snow depths below, large holes showing
their discovered resting place. Sandy who was
then just behind me called to me:

"Better dismount here. It will be safer to make
it on foot."

It was too narrow and slippery to risk on horseback. My pony boy held the bridle while I slid
off, and my own two cautious feet in hobnailed

boots aided by my khud stick helped me over that
bad place with greater safety. Then I was up on
Lalla's back again, to face more mounting on rock
ledges with the mist now almost concealing the
depths below, now blown away and starkly revealing them.

And so with many "Kabardars" and "ahistas" we
reached the top, the path widened and I crossed
the wide snow beds on Lalla's back. Mounting an
embankment on the other side, we found the path
obliterated altogether, blotted out completely by
another avalanche which had left only a bit of
slanting ice along the edge of the road to cross on.
Again I slid off Lalla's back, just in time, for he
slipped and fell, nearly rolling down onto the snow
beds below. We had all that we could do to keep
our own footing and left him to the pony men who
with much tugging brought him to his feet again.
Farther along we found another wide bed of snow
to cross. We tested it carefully with each step. It
was just a blanket below which ran a wide river.
This we saw in the growing light. The snow here
never melts; I crossed over it again in September,
but it was dirty then whereas in July it was white.

Margot was now abreast of us. We trudged
along in silence.

There were many crevasses to jump. After we
had passed safely over to the other side we looked

back and saw where the open river entered the
blanket of ice and snow. The part which we had
crossed over on was only about two feet thick. We
stood some time on the other side calling and waving warnings to the pack ponies and men to keep
them away from the crevasses some of which were
quite wide enough for a pony to slip into. Fortunately there were no mishaps.

Turning then towards Leh we trod across acres
and acres of edelweiss and I remembered my school
years in the Austrian mountains when to have
picked a single edelweiss was almost to have been
classed with the immortals. And then such a wonderful sight! Thrown across the river and glistening in the now risen sun was a perfect arch of
snow under which the waters dashed headlong.
We had passed the watershed which was buried in
snow; henceforth the river flowed with us towards
Ladakh. Up until this point it had rushed back
to the Vale of Kashmir. . . .

The road to Leh after crossing the Zoji-Là is
devoid of trees except the feathery willows and
occasional tamarisk and apricot trees in the few
"baghs" near which cluster such habitations as are
found along the road. These oases, usually ringed
in behind stone fences, afford shelter to the traveller; we sought them for that meal which, because
it is usually the only one between "chota hazri" and

dinner, has been dubbed "brunch" by English travellers.

We were in the barren lands . . . the frontier of Tibet. Although there were no more flowers along the road, high among the wild ridges were still to be seen vestiges of yellow plant life clinging to crevices in the rocks and gleaming in the sun as if Midas had swept his hand across the cliffs.

How can writers speak of those mountains as bleak or forbidding? There is a majesty about them—an aloofness, a mystery that always attaches to lonely places, but could pastel pink blending to French grey, chased by lavender and the blue of a robin's egg be forbidding? Could a skyline as changeable as an April mood be tiresome? Could peaks literally hurling themselves into the sky at any angle be monotonous? There was not a mile of the road that spelled anything but enchantment and change—change so swift that time and again it took my breath away.

If your contacts with life have been few, your joys unshared, your sorrow only for yourself; if you are afraid of the completeness of living, then the road would be voiceless to you. For those high hills have *lived*. Young though the Himalayas are among the mountains of the world, their growth has been a fervid thing that reared them high above all obstacles. And if they flaunt colours beyond the dreams of rainbows it is because deep in their hearts are precious things and because their towers and their turrets and their castle walls are the evidence of dominion.

Along these lonely stretches came traders from far Yarkand with their zos laden with bales of goods; the animals swayed on their short legs, their great horns moving from side to side as they plodded along and their long black hair glistening in the sun like spun silk. There were sheep too by the hundreds grazing in the open spaces on the sparse grass of rocky slopes, and among them, as in human herds—the goats.

We did not stop at Matchoi glacier which rears above the dak bungalow there at 17,686 feet but pushed on nine miles farther to Matayan, a distance of fifteen miles from our last stage at Baltal but still one hundred and eighty miles from Leh. Overhead the sky was cloudless and the sun pitiless. Even through dark glasses my eyes were strained and but for my gargoyle costume I could scarcely have weathered its rays.

Our pony men broke into a chant as they trudged along with the caravan close behind us. A tumble of rude huts loomed on the horizon. Matayan! This was a welcome sight in the windswept plain at 10,430 feet, for we had made a drop of over eight hundred feet since Matchoi. It was a long

SOME OF THE CREVASSES WERE QUITE WIDE ENOUGH FOR A PONY TO SLIP INTO.

BRIDGES WERE SHAKY AFFAIRS
OF RAILLESS PLANKS,

hot trek across the plain before we entered the compound through a small opening in the stone wall, a wall topped with carcasses of zos and ponies, one little brown leg still covered with hair sticking up as if in protest.

A violent battle of words raged around us as our pack ponies were unloaded and started to graze on the sparse grass within the compound.

"You must drive the ponies into the hills," the "chowkidar" was protesting.

"There is no grass there . . . it is all rock."

"They will find roots among the rocks like all the other ponies who come here."

"The sahibs cannot wait for us to catch them in the morning. They make an early start. The sahibs get very angry if we are not ready in time."

But the ruse did not work. And indeed what would be left of the grass that the owner counted on for his own horses if even one pack train were allowed to graze inside the fence? The survival of the fittest is the law of the road, and our ponies were as usual driven up into the hills to find what roots or blades of grass might survive in that austerity.

The whitewashed walls of the dak bungalow were smoked from many fires, but it was clean and I drew my charpoy out onto the porch to sleep in the bracing air. My blankets had been sewed up to form a sleeping bag, a thing unobtainable in India. My long fur-lined sleeping socks and padded robe kept out the wind and cold. Every muscle ached after the eight and a half hours of steady climbing with nerves so tense. I felt as I sometimes do after an encounter with monthly bills has dotted my check book with too many casualties: I wanted to call a "Waffenstillstand". . . Truce is too brief a word to express it. I wanted to lie down and shut my eyes for a long, long time. I wanted very much not to have to move on again next day. Yet dawn found us once more on the march through that wide plain.

CHAPTER VI

ON TO DRAS AND TO SHIMSHI KHARBU

We left Matayan about six o'clock the next morning, crossed a bridge and followed the left bank of the Dras River into the Village of Dras which lies in another wind-swept plain at 10,660 feet. We descended gradually through open country with sometimes streams to ford, then mounted along narrow paths overhanging the river. The rocks were polished like fine granite and were brown, green, and black—entirely different from any we had yet seen along the road.

At one point the river, deep down between the rocks, strained madly at its adamantine barrier, carving a path among the boulders and leaving them jutting up like the fairy castles seen in gold-fish bowls. It achieved its freedom some distance farther on where it flowed onto a wide valley near the village of Dundalthang.

Dras villages are scattered over the fertile valley, and here live those hardy Dards and Baltis who have made history for the countryside as fascinating as the record of Cortez. They have few needs,

and almost all that the outside world contributes to
them is tobacco, tea and sugar. Along the road
whenever we met men of any race the request was
for "ma-a-ches," matches. Around Dras the women wear sunbonnets for all the world like those
of our grandmothers' days and they sow crops of
buckwheat, pease, barley and lucerne in May and
reap the harvest in August. We made the twelve
and a half miles in five and a half hours of desperately hot trekking and entered a wide compound
where were serai, post and telegraph offices, the
second on our route since leaving Ganderbal. The
dak bungalow looked like a neglected barn, un-
promising from the outside and badly planned but
roomy and comfortable within. It was the sole
survival along the road of an architectural type
that has been discarded for the square structures
described. At Dras we had no dressing room.
There were two bedrooms and a dining room to the
right and two bedrooms to the left of the front hall.
This led into a roomy kitchen. It was the best room
in the building and I fancy the entire population
must gather there for shelter during those cruel
months when pitiless winds and snow make of Dras
a prototype of the Buddhist Cold Hell.

We found the bungalow cheerless. Little light
penetrated through the small windows set in walls
that were two feet thick. We had no wood for fires

and none was procurable. There are few trees in the countryside around Dras. The compound lies in a sandy, rocky plain flanked by a granary, serai, post and telegraph office. It was interesting to watch the postmaster holding hand scales up and weighing letters and my films against pieces of iron. All of this apparatus is kept in a hole in the plank floor when not in use.

Here I had to part with Lalla and with all of the other ponies of the bandobast, the Res Rules being strict in that regard. We could hold the new outfit over the next stage of Shimshi Kharbu and on into Kargil, but thereafter every dawn would see us starting out with a new transport as supplies grew scarcer, the road harder, and men and ponies had to return to their starting place for food.

I hated so to part with Lalla; and I hated to part with my "syce." Don't picture to yourself such a groom as you are familiar with. Unless he be the private servant of a sahib who supplies his uniform the syce is a man in rags and it never occurs to him to help you mount or dismount; you slide off and get on the best way you can though he stands at the pony's head and holds the reins and then trudges ahead or behind as you ordain. I kept him ahead of me after he had several times prodded my pony with a khud stick, looking quite innocent when I turned to see what could have made Lalla leap forward suddenly. But I was used to him; he was so smiling and so willing, and now all my fears and antipathies awoke. . . .

Several horses were brought in for me to try out that afternoon. They had high cossack saddles decorated with brass, and cruppers of etched brass gay with tiny flags. I brought a similar one with all its trappings home with me from Leh. It had come from Lhasa and is of sharkskin bound with damascene, the crupper decorated with flags of red and green, and its broad stirrups of damascene work. Mounted on a teak stand with the proper Chinese saddle rugs it makes an interesting addition to the furnishings of my library. I rode it for awhile on my return journey just to see if I felt as important as it looked. I did, perched high and as comfortable as in an arm chair. But for every day service I decided in favour of the lower and less impressive saddle that I had used for the first days of the journey.

I selected as Lalla's substitute an iron grey mare because of its important-looking saddle of red lacquer inset with ivory in finely worked design. The front of it was mounted high and curved as Yark-andi saddles all are. I mounted with great pride and then recalled the saying that if pride goeth before a fall it vanishes more quickly after one, and I clung desperately to the high front as the gay

PACKING UP AT KARGIL.

PONY MEN GATHERED TO BE PAID OFF. IT WAS INTERESTING TO
WATCH THEIR EXPRESSIONS.

little "tat" dashed up the slope at a gait that terrified me, and then refused to go down again at all. I thought that if one of us had to be stubborn it might as well be I so I transferred to a golden brown pony that Margot from her vantage point on the porch indicated:

"Since you are selecting your mounts for the looks of their saddles why not try that one?"

I mounted. A touch of my heavy boot and the pony cavorted. I called for help. Sandy came to his head and made the "get up" noise which means exactly the opposite out there. The pony quieted down.

"Never touch a hill pony with your boot," he advised. "They are used only to the touch of felt shoes or bare feet." He carried me well, the plump little Balti, willing and sure footed, but his "tummy" was so fat that the girths would not fit and had to be strapped on just behind his forelegs which threw the saddle too far forward for comfort. A tumble would have driven me a bit farther along the road than I cared to go in so short a time. Of all the ponies I had between Dras and Leh he was the best and I had him brought into Leh for my return journey in September. . .

The rising sun tipped just one peak of snow that showed between rifts of barren rock as we mounted next morning along a ridge where stone tablets carved with the image of Buddha flanked the roadside. Gradually the indescribable colours of the mountains were lifted from the shadows. It was cold at dawn but already at half past seven I had to take refuge in the life-saving raiment I had always close at hand, carried in a canvas bag by Happy or a coolie.

Nothing that I took with me gave me more service than that bag.

For miles we trekked down a wide valley. I on my pony, Margot and Sandy abreast of me on foot. My pony boy halted and cast himself in the dust, then raised his joined hands:

"Allah! Allah! There is no God but God!"

And we call them Infidels!

"They are fanatics. Your most devoted servant is apt to cut your throat if he finds you sleeping with your feet towards Mecca," said Sandy.

"You might live among these people forever and never know them," he continued. "Take Ali for instance. I've had him for ten years. Once when I was ill he never left me; slept on the floor beside me; brought me food. But I might have died and he would never have nursed me; would never have given me the personal care that illness demands. He stopped at the line drawn by his caste."

"He seems devoted to you," I remarked.

"I think sometimes that he is, but I never can

tell. I think that he has a sense of duty. He was magnificent in the war . . . got the cross and all that. Hides it and is shy if you mention it. He seems to take everything for granted.

"Karma!" I ejaculated.

"Perhaps. Yet he seems to feel responsible for me . . . wrote my mother once in English fashioned by the town scribe that she must not send me so much money; that it was not good for me."

Clouds cast varying shadows along the mountains. We saw never a bird, nor a flower. There was a good road up and down embankments, a bit monotonous until we came face to face with a lovely picture. Silhouetted against the sky, there on the crest of a hill before us was a man in flowing red robes mounted high on a Yarkandi saddle gay with brass trappings and heaped with brilliant saddle rugs. His head was held high; he looked over the countryside as if it were his own property; the long toes of his shoes curved upwards, their gold threads catching the glint of sunlight. At a respectful distance behind rode two women completely hidden with "burquas," those long white robes of the Mohamedan "purdah" women, which are gathered around a skull cap and flow to their feet with only a strip of embroidered openwork across their eyes. Women of mystery! And what charm in the mysterious! Everything in India seems to be touched

with it. Eyes hold unfathomable depths. Drums
are muffled. Street calls blend into a droning wail.
Unseen things are all about you. The passing show
seems to be but the echo of a scene that you have
just missed.

Once "down in India" while I was awaiting my
train in the station of Udaipur I had seen a purdah
cart drawn by oxen unload from behind its gold-
fringed pink curtains a woman and three young
children. The woman, her burqua drawn close,
huddled into a corner by the wall while the children
clung to her, gazing at me and calling her attention to the ungainly object in topi and short skirt
with feet encased in walking shoes. Her own
ankles were adorned with silver bangles and her
whole diminutive person jingled beneath the burqua
which she finally parted for a better view of the
mem-sahib. An enchanting vision she was, with
kohl-rimmed eyes and fabulously long lashes, a
slender nose above red, red lips that smiled at me—
Then the veil was quickly drawn as a burly man
came up and directed his possession to the closed
compartment on the train.

I remembered also the purdah woman I had seen
while "slumming" in Calcutta, creatures living behind high stone walls with even the sky closed off
lest some wary eye other than the master's might
view them. They were the chattels of the outcasts

of the earth, the lowest of the castes of India—the
Domes, not half so important to them as their
cattle, but wallowing in filth and swelling the tragic
lists of the tubercular in India. And here was the
system in force even on the lonely road to far
Ladakh. . . .

It took us four and a half hours to make the
fifteen miles to Tashgam from Dras. Just before
reaching the village we crossed a narrow bridge
high above a turbulent stream. This led into a narrow lane that runs between high walls of stone
which are really the walls of houses. Low openings
lead into windowless rooms which are closed in
winter with piles of stone. Mounds of clay on the
flat roofs are perforated with holes, chimneys which
let out the smoke and in winter time admit all the
air that is desired; for it is bitter cold here in winter and during the long months men women and
children hibernate until the snows that have banked
them in have melted.

We passed through Main Street of Tashgam
and on beyond to a walled-in garden where we
climbed the stone fence and rested throughout the
morning under the shade of tamarisk and apricot
trees while the caravan caught up with us, loads
were adjusted, and it passed on ahead of us. It
was half past nine o'clock when we arrived and the
sun was so desperately hot that we remained in the

shade there until one o'clock. Margot pulled off her shoes and stockings and bathed her feet in the stream that trickled through the garden. I lay under an apricot tree, my carryall for pillow. Sandy pounced upon the tiffin basket and spread its delights before us: Cold chicken . . . we had managed to get one in Dras, Boston baked beans . . . it is harder to tell whether they are best cold or hot. Scones, soon warmed in the sun . . . the butter already in that state.

"Shake the tree, Sandy, and we'll have dessert!"

A shower of apricots fell over us. We ate . . . and then we slept.

The sun was at the zenith of its cruelty when Sandy called out:

"We must be moving on!"

"Do wait a bit! It must be a hundred and fifty out there in the sun."

"We'll never get into Shimshi Kharbu before dark if we don't move on," exclaimed Sandy. "I for one don't relish being caught on a rock ledge after dark."

It grew hotter and hotter as the road wound up along cliffs with overhanging boulders and sometimes sudden terrifying curves above the Dras River.

"How do you two stand it," I cried. "I'd be dead if I wore light topis like yours. I feel as if

I might faint any minute as it is. My head is numb and dizzy."

"We never had brain fever . . . or sunstroke as you have," they replied.

We passed a flat-roofed hut partly built into a cliff. A low door led into the utter darkness of a single small room.

"A hermit's hut," I cried.

"Something more wonderful. The hut of a dak or mail runner," Sandy explained. "Each one speeds for his given number of miles after which he passes the sack on to the man ahead. In this way they keep open communication between Leh and the rest of the world until the snows render the service impossible. Heavy loads go in on ponies." We saw them every three miles along the road. Most of them were mere burrows in the ground, but some two roomed ones are being built that will house a man's pony as well as himself when fierce hail and snow drive them from the road. I realized that I had not quite lost touch with civilization when I saw the dak runners, recognizable by the wide brass buckles on their belts, and when at intervals I noted the telegraph poles which run out as far as Leh where they stop at the outpost of civilization. The wires are often strung along cliffs, though I did not notice any at all along the Zoji-Là.

I tried taking pictures from horse back but even

with the pony man holding the reins, the whir of the movie camera had results that nearly ended in disaster both for the camera and for me. So I was forced to dismount, and wait each time to call the pony man to hold the horse while I slid off on ledges so narrow that there was barely room for the pony and for me at the same time. Happy with my camera was usually behind when I most wanted him, but in spite of difficulties I have a wonderful record in motion pictures. . . .

It was a tedious trek of twenty-one miles from Dras to Shimshi Kharbu and already half-past three that afternoon before we reached the loveliest dak bungalow of the whole road. A porch ran around two sides of it, one side being directly above the high bank of the river which at this point was churned into rapids. Willow trees gave abundant shade and the rooms of this new structure were large. The old dak bungalow had been demolished by an avalanche during the early spring.

We dined on the porch as the setting sun touched the snow peaks with a wonderful glow. I slept outdoors, and although so tired, I was almost sorry to fall to sleep while the camp sounds trailed across the small courtyard that separated the dak bungalow from the serai where our men were polishing boots, washing out clothes, or smoking their hookahs as they rested, old Kadera a towering silhouette in the glowing doorway lit with the firelight within. There was the thud of impatient hoofs from the line of tethered ponies, the call of myriads of stars—and then oblivion.

CHAPTER VII

HALF WAY TO LEH, AT KARGIL . . . AND ON
BEYOND

UNDER a brilliant canopy of stars we resumed the march next day at four-thirty. The road ascended sharply over a spur of the Shingo Nullah which leads on up to the plains of the Deo Sai, famous for its bears and game of all sorts. It made me think of other days when I had settled into a duck blind behind the rushes before dawn with one who also loved the big outdoors. I was aware again of the stars above, of the call of our decoys as fluttering wings outlined against the lightening sky, of the silence, tense, with wild geese circling above us. And now the moonlight was so bright that even at that early hour we could discern mountain peaks which at this point tower sixteen, seventeen, eighteen thousand feet high. Here the Dras River empties into the Shiggar along which the route follows until that too blends with the Suru just before entering Kargil, at a point where a fine suspension bridge crosses into Skardo . . . the sportsman's Paradise.

The moon held long in the heavens after the sun had risen and the path wound up and down along khuds. It grew hotter and ever hotter, the mountains less colourful and friendly, and patches of purple sage strove in vain to relieve the growing austerity. My face had been badly blistered the day before; heavy applications of cold cream and liquid powder had only partly relieved the sting which grew to an ache along the scorching road to Kargil, the most tedious of all the marches. The road was diverted by a landslide and crossed many bridges, ever more sketchy affairs where lumber is scarce and they are at best doomed to early destruction in the summer floods and therefore not worth much care; narrow rickety bridges they were, with holes filled with stones which made the going harder along narrow, railless planks. Each one was a new experience in nerve-tension.

At Chanegund we had "brunch" in an apricot grove, where again we had merely to reach up and pick our dessert. It was then eight forty-five—and so hot that I sagged in my saddle with my eyes aching worse than all my muscles did. And hotter still was the road beyond which turned up a very sharp rock ladder, cutting zigzag along the face of the cliff; each bend concealed the bit of road beyond, which seemed to be a winding path through boulders under an overhanging cliff. Some

fifty feet below rushed the river and here I nearly
went over the brink as, rounding a boulder, I saw
Margot just ahead of me resting on a rock and
twirling her pongee sunshade which was lined with
green.

Sunshades are rare in those parts; probably my
Balti had never seen so strange and fearsome a
sight, and he at once gave evidence of his intention
to back away from it down the cliff into the river.
I could not turn on a path so narrow; I had outdistanced my pony man; and when I looked back
quickly to see if he might be near enough to run
forward and lead the pony past I saw him just
mounting the path around a boulder.

When he took in the situation he stood stock
still and held up his hands instead of rushing to
help me. Sandy was far on ahead. There seemed
at that moment to be only one outcome as I could
not halt my pony on the descending grade, nor
dismount. I called to Margot: "He is going to
shy at your parasol!"

Fortunately she took in the situation promptly
and at once lowered her sunshade. When we
came abreast, and the pony swerved away from the
spot, she reached out and took his rein and led
him on a few paces after which we proceeded without further trouble into Kargil.

All through those trying hours I had been

CLIFFS OF PURPLE SHALE LED DOWN TO A VALLEY.

THE TIFFIN COOLIE.

CHORTENS—RECEPTACLES FOR THE ASHES OF THE DEAD.

thinking of the peace of a dak bungalow set among shady trees. It was a bitter disappointment on reaching Kargil to find that the old one had been closed and a new one built high on a bluff on the other side of the river. This meant another weary climb on a bluff of sand after eight hours of trekking when we had covered sixteen miles.

The new bungalow was set in a wide compound with not a yard of shade and not a drop of water nearer than the river far below from whence all of our drinking and bathing water had to be hauled by Happy and the coolies. They uncomplainingly performed this task with the usual promptness, the sahibs, comfort always being their first consideration.

From Dras we had descended to 8,700 feet and to what seemed a cauldron in the burning heat and glare of midday. Kargil, the capital of Purig, is in Mohamedan country and the town of greatest importance between Srinagar and Leh. It has post and telegraph office and a number of small native shops where one may buy cloth and oil and native shoes and such oddments as one may need to patch one's outfit midway on the road. At Kargil also one's pink passes must be presented to the thesildar in order that one may secure transportation from there on to Leh. I had pictured that a thesildar would be hoary with age, a Moseslooking man, but he proved to be young, of the "babu" type so familiar down in India. He spoke English perfectly and seemed to feel the importance of his position in the community.

All of our ponies and transport men had to be paid off at Kargil where a new outfit was to be secured. The men gathered on the wide porch of the rest house while Sandy, surrounded by little leather bags containing anna bits, passed the stipulated amounts to each one in turn. For covering the two stages with us each pony man received Rs. 2.6, or about $1.10, and each coolie Rs. 1.3 or about 45 cents, and this for marching thirty-seven miles.

It was interesting to watch their expressions. They were so eager to get this pittance and so grateful for the pitiful tip which one should not exceed lest the custom of the road be broken and discontent ensue. They looked spellbound at the little leather pouches from which the annas were drawn. They knew of course that we did not carry so heavy and cumbersome a load on our persons and that therefore this seeming wealth must have been in the yakdans they had guarded along the road; yet such a thing as theft would never occur to them. And here was a mixture of races: Dards, Mongolians, Baltis, Ladakhis, having no possible loyalty to us personally. Yet we could trust every one of them . . .

Kargil being midway to Leh, one takes time there to sort his baggage and check up supplies. The men seemed to have taken inventory of their ailments likewise and there was generous distribution of eye lotion, cough mixture and Eno's fruit salts. It looked for a time also as if we were to have an interesting surgical case which was prepared for with such attention to sanitation as would have edified the doctors. A table composed of boxes of tinned goods piled one upon the other was covered with a clean pillow case; this was not sterilized of course, for it had ridden the ranges in my bedding roll, but it was white and impressive-looking. On it I deposited peroxide, iodine, antiseptic gauze, bandages and shears the while our patient eyed us with what I thought was admiration. He had come to us with a lump on his neck as large as a hen's egg and this was to be opened by Sandy with a needle run through a cork to prevent it from entering too far.

The needle was properly run through a flame and Sandy was ready to perform the operation while I took up an advantageous position with my camera to "chart" the case, when our patient decided that he preferred the evil that he had become familiar with. As he would have none of the needle we gave him some castor oil instead. He was just as well satisfied.

We decided to start in the afternoon next day and break the long stage of twenty-three miles by pitching our tents at Paskyum some seven miles farther along the road where there was a good camping ground. We had our first experience with fractious ponies as our caravan was loading in the afternoon. When some of the ponies were led up to the neatly stacked loads they began bucking and rearing, and when the packs were strapped on after much trouble they were at once dislodged or thrown off before they could be made secure. The ponies lay down and rolled to prevent reloading.

I eyed my new white pony suspiciously. He probably thought as little of me as I did of him, and neither of us grew fonder of the other during the hours on the road. A girth buckle broke when it was being tightened; the breast strap had got packed with the equipment and my saddle slipped backwards constantly as we mounted. The crupper was a flimsy, loose rope to which I clung miserably when the descent was steep and the pony was so thin that the saddle did not fit at all. Altogether I was too uncomfortable to enjoy the scenery as we set out in a drizzle of rain at

THE WRITER WITH KHUD STICK.

SURELY NOTHING ELSE THAN A WORLD GONE MAD—CLIFFS OF
ORANGE, BLUE, PURPLE, RED, PILING UP, EVER MORE
JAGGED IN OUTLINE.

PERCHED HIGH ON A ROCK THAT
RAN UP ALMOST TO A POINT
WAS THE FIRST LAMASERY
—MOULBE.

STONES OF EVERY SIZE AND COLOUR EACH ONE WITH THE MANTRA OF TIBET
CUT DEEP INTO IT. "OM MANÉ PADME HUM."

five o'clock on the road which mounted over a wide plateau. I was too sorry for myself to think of the pony's feelings, but looking back on that ride I'm sure he must have been wishing that I would remain in the same spot between his head and tail. I wished that I could. The saddle wouldn't let me; it preferred that I should spend most of my time over his tail or on his neck. There was one very steep descent, then at half-past six we jumped the ponies across a sluice that marked off a small bagh shaded with willow trees where our tents were soon pitched beside the river, at this point the Wakka.

Before it grew dark we had time to inspect some interesting subterranean flour mills located near our camp; we crawled through low openings into an underground room from where we looked down on to the channel of a stream which, on its way to join the river, turned a mill wheel. The ground around our bagh was seamed with rivulets, which could be closed off or let loose at will by the placement or removal of stones or mud dams. During the night one of the sluices was opened above our camp and down went Margot's tent pole while my flashlight showed a rivulet coursing through my tent and threatening to undermine my tent pole also.

Our ever-willing men were soon about with

lanterns, closed the sluice and straightened tent poles, so the worse result was a sore throat from sleeping in so much dampness. The next day Happy developed a toothache, a complaint that we were not armed against. Sandy decided that a little Coué treatment and tooth paste mixed with water would do as well. Happy declared next day that it had cured him.

Paskyum is a picturesque place and has contributed its bit to history. The summits of the mountains about are tipped with forts for there was constant inter-tribal warfare when the Ladakhis resisted the invasions of the Dogras. One ruin in particular looked very romantic in the dusk towering on an isolated peak but indistinctly seen through a drizzle of rain. That rain forced us to finish under the wide fly of my tent the dinner we had begun under a willow tree by the river bank.

CHAPTER VIII

INTO LAMALAND

"I SHALL sleep in Lamaland to-night." That was my first thought on awakening July 29th. Dressing by the faint flare of a lantern filled with diluted oil from Kargil was more difficult than usual, or was it because I was excited with the promise of a wonderful day? We were on the road at four o'clock. It was too dark and too slippery to mount at once, for the path was barely visible. Coolies carried us on their backs over the wide sluice and we made our several ways across rivulets swollen from the night's rain and glistening now in brilliant moonlight.

Once out from under the banks and the trees, we needed no lanterns to find the way. It was light enough, even after we entered a gorge, to see the cliffs silhouetted in fantastic forms against a gradually lightening sky, and sunrise broke over orange-coloured sandstone. The sky was of clearest blue. Wheat fields and a river were on our right as the road mounted embankments then went on to a high khud with some bad going over boul-

der and rock-strewn paths until it led to a wide
plain.   Then down, down, down, it went in sharp
drops and on up again to rock shelves, winding,
winding along the mountain face, narrow and steep.
I rode, as usual, until I was stiff from the saddle,
then trudged on foot as long as I was able to.   In
this way I managed to get on well and even without acquiring blisters.

Cliffs of purple shale led down to a valley.
Farther along they were bright red with patches
of orange fungus like beauty spots upon them, and
the road was lined with huge bushes of Rose of
Sharon and wild roses, then past their bloom but
drooping great pods of red.   The sand under foot
was deep purple, then red where shale had pow-
dered and mingled with the dust of the road; and
the shale of the overhanging rocks beside the road
stood up vertically like the thin pages of a book,
split by the intense extremes of heat and cold; one
could pick them out in sections as I did.   Even
now as I write I can look at the souvenirs that
would otherwise seem unbelievable memories of
blending colours.

In the fields were now strange people; women
with wide flaps of black astrakhan, like elephant's
ears, spreading on each side of their faces; a strip
of leather covered with red cloth heavily studded
with huge turquoise running from a point above

their forehead, widening out over the crowns of their heads and narrowing gradually below the waist. This was the much-discussed "peyrak" said to represent a cobra, being a relic of snake worshipping days. Sometimes an extra strip at the side turned upwards, studded with coral, to simulate its tail. From their ears hung long earrings of seed pearls; on their wrists were wide white shell cuffs, and their garments were of maroon or dark blue homespun. These were the polyandrous women of Ladakh who take unto themselves several brothers of a family when they marry one . . .

We stopped for brunch in a shady spot beside the river overhung by a natural cave. Our usual method was for the one ahead to stop at the first convenient spot about eight-thirty and wait for the others to join up. Travellers along this road sometimes make camp at Durkit or at Lotsun, but we found it easy to cover the sixteen miles from Paskyum to Moulbe and more pleasant to settle in a comfortable dak bungalow whence it is also easier to get started in the morning, having no tents to pack up . . .

At Shergol we saw the first "chorten." These are receptacles for the ashes of the dead which are mixed with clay and pounded into varying shapes like cakes that have been irreverently termed "potted lamas." The chortens themselves are of many shapes, the base sometimes round, but more often square, enormous in size and surmounted with a round dome from which in most cases a high red spire runs up in thirteen tiers representative of the thirteen Bodisat heavens. The base is always whitewashed and sometimes fantastically painted. From Shergol all the way to Leh chortens are seen in great numbers, sometimes in rows of various shapes and sizes, sometimes at each end of "mané" walls. These are more impressive still as they run through desert stretches standing about six feet in height with sloping or flat top and always covered with stones of every size and colour each one with the mantra of Tibet cut deep into it: "Om mané padme hum," literally translated as: "Oh God, the Jewel in the Lotus" . . .

Books had somewhat prepared me for a grand sight before entering Moulbe, or Maulba Chamba as it is also called, but I suppose one cannot be prepared for a fourth dimension; one enters into it as into "samadhi," that visionary state of the Indian mystic. Suddenly at a turn of the road I was looking out over what could surely be nothing else than a world gone mad, unthinkable, impossible to picture until seen. It satisfied the pagan in me. Across a wide, wide valley which lay far down below the road and where the Wakka ran

through green fields, rose cliffs of orange, blue,
purple, red, piling up higher and higher, ever in
more jagged outline as if gathering force from a
fierce impetus that hurled them into the sky. They
were bent this way and that with great seams rent
in their sandstone cliffs by ice and snow and burning heat. Topping these were still higher peaks,
snow clad, the crests of all broken into a million
lances. I reined in my pony, gazing breathlessly
at the picture of such force and power.

Big moments that I had lived and that endured
in memory came flooding back . . . moments of
power:

Chanel in the strength of her beauty, draped in
the tricolour of France; her head thrown back; that
most sublime of martial airs drowning even the
notes of a full orchestra as her voice rose higher
and higher until the audience wept with emotion:

"Marchons!   Marchons!"   The   legions   of
France seemed to pass before us.

Then striking the very depths of tenderness, a
voice that was now soft as the rustle of leaves:
"Amour sacré de la patrie."

That picture faded. Another came . . .

Out of the stillness of the night a clarion cry:
"Garde à vous!" Pompiers dashed through Paris
streets. It was January 1916. The sky was
overcast. With many others I rushed out into

the street, a fur coat over my nightclothes. One
did such things in Paris in those days. We stood
in the Place de l'Opéra . . . a silent throng. The
streets were dark. Faint glimmers only touched
the pavements where occasional street lamps
flickered under their war bonnets.

A terrific crash. A bomb had fallen. Where?
It sounded near enough. Would the next one
find us huddled there?

Silence. The sky was clearing. There was a
bright star above. But no! The whir of an
engine came down to us faint as a whispered
prayer.

Again memory's picture changed:

A typhoon lashed the water behind my bungalow at Zamboanga in the Philippines. It rose
steadily. Soon it covered the sea wall. There
was eight feet of it in my house. Later we caught
fishes there. Earth was obliterated. The Army
post seemed to be a collection of Noah's Arks
floating on the ocean. Even by screaming one
could not make oneself heard above the rush of
wind.

That was power . . . and here was power incarnate in rock.

It was ruthless Power . . . but also Harmony.

Colour is sound to me, and here was no sensuous
thrill of a Venusberg, nor the measured tread of a

Pilgrims' Chorus but the mad scarlet notes that lift you to intense suspense on the crashing waves of a great symphony. What a vision for their Creator when they soared to meet Him in the sky! For the first time in my life I gleaned some understanding of God the Father—the Great Jehovah of the Old Testament. Here was Jehovah in all His might, all powerful, all seeing, no throne so worthy of Him. He ceased to be to me what until then He had been, only a face with long, flowing beard, remote above the clouds as the Holy Pictures represent Him. . . .

Over golden sandstone the road wound easily down. There, at a turn, perched high on a rock that ran up almost to a point, was the first lamasery or monastery whose monks are known as lamas in this strange land. And this was Moulbe. Between rice and wheat fields the road descends to the dak bungalow. In the fields were women with babies strapped to their backs or carried in baskets, or nestling in the folds of shawls tied across their mothers' breasts, the little heads swaying to and fro as the women moved about the fields. All children are precious in Ladakh where polyandry restricts the birth rate . . .

A sharp drop of the road and we were in the compound at Moulbe and objects of curiosity for the lamas and men of the village gathered there.

We found a fierce altercation going on while our ponies were being unloaded; translated, the argument registered an old man's complaint that bad as it was to have his fields trodden by our horses it was far worse to be insulted by a mere boy such as our pony man. He was told to thrash the boy and take his revenge, but whether satisfied with his victory or overcome with religious qualms he answered: "No—God will punish him!"

How I regretted all along the road that I could not speak the language of the countryside. There was so much that I wanted to find out and never could, for here even Urdu was useless.

Ragged, filthy, cheerful, these Ladakhis were. The lamas wore three-quarter length homespun coats of wine colour and somewhat Chinese cut, fastened across the breast and falling loosely, held in by a wide sash of red which was wound many times around the waist. This held all sorts of odds and ends from artistic metal and leather flint cases to spoons, pen boxes of silver, and artistic locks and keys that looked more like ornaments than things of common utility. I brought several of these home with me. And what a receptacle the robe itself! Wide inside pockets front and back with capacity for all the needs of the road and usually bulging at all angles and hiding what is a fine slim figure. The lamas wore high boots, the others anything they had managed to fashion, probably made out of the skins of such animals as had dropped by the roadside, the rawhide being gathered over the foot and sewed to a wide ankle band of felt. Some of these were gaily embroidered. I found a pair of new ones in Leh, elaborate affairs of many colours. Most of the men had their legs from ankle to knee wound about with strips of felt held in place with black tape that gives an artistic striped effect. On their heads, worn at any angle, were crush hats with what must once have been upstanding crowns about four inches high with pointed ear flaps of astrakhan curled or drooping according to the degree of its age and infirmity.

Battered, ragged, patched and dirty all their garments were, but with them were always worn turquoise earrings, loops of silver set with turquoise, necklaces of turquoise and carnelian, and rings and bracelets, many of these with snake heads on the ends. Thus my ragged pony man was garbed, and I noted a streak of grease down the middle of his back where his long braid of frowsy hair had rubbed for years.

CHAPTER IX

ACROSS THE NAMIKA LÀ AT 13,180 FEET

IT was overcast and raining when we marched out of Moulbe next morning at four. The next stop was Bod Kharbu sixteen miles distant. Again I walked with Margot and Sandy until dawn, then mounted my new pony, this time an iron grey, a dapper and fleet little beast with an easy running walk. We soon outdistanced the others, and I was left alone on a sandy plain with my little pony boy who shuffled ahead at a fast gait although burdened with my carryall and my movie camera. He was the merriest little soul imaginable, hair escaping at every angle from under his battered cap, his garment patched in so many places that hardly any of the original material was left. But the inevitable turquoise earrings decorated his ears and he wore the ring that none seemed to be too poor to purchase . . .

Round knolls of sandstone spread over a wide valley, then the road narrowed and mounted gradually on a sandy embankment between barren hills. Everything was sand colour—and how

RANGES THAT SOARED AS IF THE WHOLE WORLD HAD RISEN AT ONCE
—A WORLD WITHOUT CITIES OR VILLAGES OR OCEANS. SEEN
FROM THE TOP OF THE NAMIKA-LÀ 13,180 FEET
—AT DAWN.

THE PEAKS WERE PUSHING AND SHOVING EACH OTHER AS IN THE MAD
SCRAMBLE OF A FOOT-BALL GAME.

CAVE EYES LOOKED DOWN FROM VERTICAL FISSURES—THE
LAMASERY AT LAMAYURU.

WE LOOKED OUT OVER RANGES MORE COLOURFUL THAN THE STAINED GLASS
WINDOWS OF A CHURCH—DAWN ON THE FOTU-LÀ, 13,446 FEET.

silent! Only the thud of my pony's hoofs and
the flap, flap of the boy's leather shoes, far too big
for him, registered in that immense desolation.
For miles and miles we wandered on alone, no
sign of life about, no blade of grass, no tree, no
flower, no bird, no drop of water.

I usually carried my vest pocket camera slung
around my neck when on horseback, and just here
it suddenly struck the saddle and frightened the
pony who bolted, nearly throwing me. Strangely
enough I was not afraid; it happened so quickly
and on an up grade so that he tired soon; the road
was wide at that point, well over a yard, and the
drop to the left not deep and at a slope which
never seemed so bad as when it fell sheer down.
Sandy argued with me later that it would be better
to drop straight off a khud and finish the job at
once rather than roll down with the possibility of
escape at the price of maiming. I had no answer
to this except "I prefer slopes." I think the pony
believed me when I patted him and assured him,
"I will never do it again," for we travelled ahead
without further trouble, the scared pony boy sticking now close beside him.

There was too much sameness of colouring, a
drab yellowness of sand like some women's hair
that just will not glint even in the sunlight. The
road made a sharp up grade zigzag and there I

was at dawn on the top of the Namika Là at
13,180 feet with all about me the vigour of wide,
wild ranges. Was there such a thing as civilization anywhere? Where was the world that I had
once known . . . full of so many people and so few
individuals? What was Time itself? A mere
name that we could hitch things on to that we
called "seasons" just as we marked our miles back
there with milestones and our stages out here with
dak bungalows.

The Namika Là does not mean Salt Pass, as
it is sometimes given, but "Pillar of the Sky" in
Ladakhi. Just where I stood on its crest a Lhato
with some worn prayer flags fluttering from its pile
of stones marked the pass. Such piles of stones are
seen often on mountain peaks, erected to propiti-
ate the demons of the passes. At the summit I
dismounted and took photographs. I gazed
down onto a wide valley and out over ranges that
soared as if the whole world had risen at once, a
world without cities or villages or oceans, only
mountains untouched by the foot of man . . . and
these so high.

Turning to look back I found the west glowing
with the reflection of all the gorgeous colours of
the rising sun. The sun itself is never seen at
dawn or sunset in these high altitudes, only the
stage effects of its lantern colours thrown over the

mountains. Some reared crests of pink, some
billowed lavender and blue in the shadows, and
toward the East where my path lay, dark ranges
chased with clouds were flung higher, higher,
higher. And because I stood so high myself on
this Pillar of the Sky and my view was unob-
structed I seemed to look out over peaks that
towered up to twenty thousand feet. And they
will tell you out here that the Ladakh range is low;
that it only averages 3,500 feet higher than Mt.
Blanc while beyond and farther north runs the
greatest mass of mountains in the world, the Karakorum which hides K-2. And when those who
love the mountains out here say "K-2" their voice
has a tender note. For K-2 is a purdah lady and
the lovers who have seen her face are only the
very brave who deserve the fair. One of these
when autographing his book for me wrote:
"Maybe you will see K-2." That indeed would
be worth the most strenuous trip. But I did not
see K-2, and life seems less complete for having
missed that great experience . . .

From where I stood, looking east, jagged rock
chased jagged cliff into the sky, some tearing off
veils of snow which lay in the spaces of their dark
clefts. I wanted to linger, but it was a quarter to
eight and growing very hot; so I mounted and
rode slowly down the gradual descent through a

land that looked as if God had swept His hand
across it in anger and then forgot it. The enormous silence of a still mid-ocean as you see it from
the lookout at night encompassed everything. It
was like the monstrous darkness that comes to a
man suddenly gone blind, a bewildered and hopeless thing with memories and regrets but never a
hope. Beyond the dark spaces toward which I was
headed lay surely all of the eight Buddhist Hells.
Dante must have seen them before he wrote
"Inferno."

It grew very hot as I descended. Happy joined
me here having come on ahead of the bandobast.
We passed a few huts, then on through more
desolation, no flower or shrub or tree; then deep
mud to wade through, Happy and the pony boy
holding their boots high. And beyond the peaks
were pushing and shoving each other as in the mad
scramble of a football game. I hoped to find a bit
of shade to wait in while the others caught up with
me, but it was in burning sun that I finally sat
down and, when Margot and Sandy came up a half
hour later, we had that indefinite meal called
brunch. But it was too hot to linger. They moved
on ahead, and I followed slowly through the for-
gotten land, loving to be alone where there were
no khuds. Some Ladakhi traders passed and
their "zhu-le" I now answered promptly with

IN THE VILLAGE LANES AT KHALATSI.

GROUP OF MEN AND WOMEN HAVING TEA IN THE FIELD.

WE STRUCK SHEER UP THE FACE OF A CLIFF.

THE PONIES FELL TIME AND AGAIN TO THEIR KNEES AS THEY WERE PUSHED AND
PULLED UP BY THE PONY MEN.

"zhu." They wore goatskins flung across their shoulders to protect them from the sun's rays as my spine pad protected me.

Then up and down, up and down I went, along broken, crumbling ledges. I was nervous again for it looked as if surely the edge would give under the combined weight of the pony and myself. It was so useless to coax him from the edge. Such a strange country! Seeming to wait for something that never happened. And the river shown on my map was called the Sangeloomah. I thought that altogether the appropriate name for it; for just there a pony, turned out to graze, had his entire side raw and bleeding . . .

When I returned over the Namika Là in September nothing was the same. I rose to the pass with those deep shadows behind me while the sun made bright the hills ahead. Or was it because, riding then a swift horse, I swept up the wide spaces chatting the while and so losing the sound of other more mysterious voices? . . .

Entering Bod Kharbu where we were to rest for the night, we saw the first chortens and mané walls worth recording, indeed quite the best ones of the whole route. They are the first things to be seen on entering every village and the last on leaving it as they form the approach from both sides. They are impressive. Hundreds and hundreds of stones are piled on top of a wall six or eight feet wide, some of them standing upright, a few painted with the image of Buddha but most of them with only the mantra of Tibet carved once or as many times as the space allows: "Om mané padme hum!" "O God, the Jewel in the Lotus!" Hosannas and Hallelujahs of Tibet.

It is strange to our western ears, this voice that rises in the wilderness, that goes up from every corner of that mysterious land, from every throat, from thousands of prayer wheels and prayer flags that top the walls of temples and of houses: "Om mané padme hum!" And why so strange this testimony to His greatness; this song of praise that runs up incessantly from all over the highest land in the world — the nearest to His throne? So insistent is the cry, so persistent, so multiple, so strong in its united force. It is novel merely because it comes to us along a new avenue of associations, a familiar thought clothed in an unfamiliar label. Do we not burn candles that flicker night and day before some shrine for special intentions? Do we not see votive offerings in Christian churches—hear songs of praise too for particular benefits? Do we not cry to heaven constantly for special blessings and privileges much in the same spirit as that in which the Buddhist twirls his prayer wheel or lays his prayer stone upon the wall that crops may be better, or floods less severe, or that the friend journeying across these dangerous passes may return in safety?

In that interesting book, "The Buddhist Praying Wheel," William Simpson explains the mystery which surrounds this much-discussed mantra, identifying it with the symbols under which Siva is worshipped throughout India. The lotus having a sexual symbolism, the Creative Force of the universe is hereby extolled, the actual words of the mantra being, according to the Sacred Books of the East, expressions of the reproductive power, Padma or Lotus the female, Mané, the Jewel, the male. Simpson gives many examples to show how widespread this particular form of symbolism was at the early period of the world when the mantra of Tibet is supposed to have originated. The Lotus Flower floats on the water, detached from earth. In Genesis the Spirit of God is described as moving on the face of the waters at the beginning of all things. Indian art represents Vishnu as floating on the waters and from his umbilicus issues a lotus stalk on the flower of which sits Brahma in the act of creating all things. Horus too sits on his throne in the midst of waters. The Druids held the mistletoe sacred because it had no roots in the polluted earth.

And because they have not yet seen the light

that has come to a Western world they are as full of
fear of the Unseen as we are full of fear of the unseen world "On the Other Side." Thus the song of
praise is blended with the hope of protection. For
them still lingers the Evil Eye which we of the
West put out when we burned our last witches.
For that reason they put a dab of red paint on the
corner of their houses and hang a ram's skull with
horns attached over the door to frighten demons
away. If for demons of earth it is pointed down-
wards, and if for those of the air it must be a dog's
skull facing upwards, and the forehead should be
painted with ochre. If they have lost many children and another precious mite comes to them in
the land where children are scarce they may call
him Drogpa, for then the demons will say: "We
won't pay any attention to that one; he is
only a Nomad."

Are there not people claiming western enlight-
enment who will not undertake a journey on
Friday; who dread the thirteenth, who would not
sit thirteen at table or wear peacock's feathers?
And do we not throw a pinch of the salt that we
have spilled over our left shoulder? And should
one not make a wish when the new moon is first
seen over his left shoulder? And haven't we
"Santa Claus," though he may come down to
modern children from an aeroplane instead of

jingling his bells across the roof? We ourselves aren't weaned from all that delectable make-believe that is none the less alluring because refutable. So why do we wonder and even make fun of the still more understandable childish fancies of a people who are land-locked between high mountain ranges where the march of progress has not trodden their beliefs into the dust? It makes the whole countryside more interesting if one tries to understand them . . .

"Mirror of Justice; Seat of Wisdom, Spiritual Vessel; Mystical Rose; Tower of David; House of Gold; Morning Star—Pray for us! From Thy anger. From all evil. From the Power of the Devil, O Lord deliver us. That Thou spare us, we beseech Thee to hear us!" This is a Catholic Prayer.

"O, Give us such blessings as will clear away the sins of defilement and bad deeds. Bless us with mental guidance. Bless us by cutting us off from worldly illusion. Bless us by putting us on the right path. Bless us by causing us to understand all things. Bless us to be useful to each other with kindliness. Bless us to know ourselves thoroughly. Bless us to be mild from the depths of our hearts. Bless us to be brave as Yourself." This is a Buddhist Prayer. . . .

I rode down beside the mané walls careful to

keep them on my right to "gain merit," and I passed through village lanes level with the house-tops whereon floated prayer flags, and on down to the tiny dak bungalow at Bod Kharbu at 11,000 feet. And here also the mountains soared like bent organ pipes.

At Bod Kharbu I was badly bitten by fleas, no disgrace in India where they are mentioned quite naturally in the vernacular of curses. I wondered how the men fared huddled around the camp fires in lodgings that must have encouraged hordes of such visitors.

CHAPTER X

CROSSING THE FOTU LÀ AT 13,446 FEET, AND INTO LAMAYURU

THE march could not be resumed at dawn next day. Indeed it looked as if we were to be marooned indefinitely in Bod Kharbu as the stream, once easily crossed on a narrow bridge which had been washed away, was now a torrent fed by a spate from the mountains near by. All landmarks were obliterated and Kadera seemed dubious about our chances of getting across ourselves, much less of landing the laden pack ponies safely on the other side.

"And there is another stream beyond," he said. "We might find ourselves between two of them with no shelter or food and no telling how for long." He spoke in Urdu. Sandy translated.

We retreated disconsolately to the porch of the rest house. At nine o'clock came the click of little hoofs against stones; our fresh ponies coming up the road . . . and from across the swollen stream.

"Shall we try it?" This from Sandy.

"Yes . . . let's!" This from me.

We hurried down to the bank and noticed where the ponies struck the shallowest parts. Better a wetting than to sit still in Bod Kharbu with Leh still eighty miles away. So we started out. The next stage was fifteen miles distant.

A new horse each morning meant for me an hour of dread as to what each one's peculiarity might develop to be. But this white one took me across the swirling waters easily and up the partly washed-out embankment on the other side where I turned him back across the stream in order that those who were walking might cross one by one with as little wetting as possible. The embankments and long sweeping slopes beyond were easy going and I was glad that I had not started on another and still better mount that had reared and plunged when his light load of carryall and raincoats was tied on, and continued to misbehave whenever anyone got near him.

It was an easy gradient up to the Fotu Là, past chortens and manés. A high wind swept the pass, and a driving rain that turned to hail ended in a thunderstorm which rolled off over the dark mountains and left all clear and beautiful by the time I reached the top of the pass at 13,446 feet a long way ahead of the others. Up a slope to the right a herd of eleven sharpoo, gazelle-like animals, were grazing peacefully, easily seen with the naked eye. From the summit I looked over crags of the most extraordinary shape, pointed like cathedral towers; I could almost hear their symphony of blue and grey and green—and why not? It would seem to be a question of vibrations and of "tuning in" since colour is produced by ether waves and sound by air waves.

The Fotu Là with its bent pinnacles of grey, blue and saffron toned down to pastel was beautiful in those early morning hours and I did not want to hurry down to the next stage, so rare a privilege was it to me, the city-caged, to climb so high. I wanted to stay long up there that its treasures might sink down into memory and the amplitude of beauty and silence abide with me. If you have known Spring Time, in places like this memories will come flooding back poignantly sweet, like youth surviving in the heart of old age, at once its salvation and its tragedy. The history of millions of years is carved upon the rocks there; struggle, growth, victory and death such as they were back at the dawn of Time before civilization had come into being.

Margot and Sandy came up. We sat down on the crest of the pass beside a Lhato from which floated torn prayer flags. We looked down upon a world that no longer touched us, and out over ranges more colourful than the stained glass windows of a church, and up to crags soaring in full-throated praise: "Jubilate Deo, universa terra: Psalmum dicite nomine ejus."

I shall always feel now that one should climb many steps to a church. The very act of mounting high uplifts one. Churches are best where the sanctuary lamp is by day the sun, by night the moon and stars, pure air the frankincense . . . the worshippers . . . silent peaks. And it seemed to me up there that men had measured God too infinitesimally small; had clipped their winged thoughts unnecessarily. Did not all prayers reach Him, whether they ascended as "Kyrie Eleison!" "Allah! Allah!" or "Om mané padme hum!"?

When I mounted my pony and fell behind Margot and Sandy as we descended, Kadera joined me and trudged beside me for some time. Now and again we made efforts at conversation; he would wave his long arm towards the north and say: "Burzil Choka!" and I would nod my head and answer: "Deo Sai." We both understood that we were planning the return trip which we intended to make that way. Smiles and nods ended our conversation; we never got any further than that.

Kadera's costume, like my own, was somewhat the worse for wear. His three-quarter length homespun coat, cut after the pattern of a frock coat gone wrong, was creased and greased and torn; his chaplies fitted none too well and where the straps had broken they were tied with bits of rope. His long stride had to adjust itself to my slower gait as we descended two thousand feet.

More chortens and manés greeted us and men in goatskin capes who smiled and said: "Zhu-le!" and sometimes even put out their tongues which is the courteous greeting in Tibet.

The road led through the bed of a stream, and to the left a strange formation of sandstone was pointed like a forest of brown pines running up the hillside. We climbed a narrow path rounding a hill and out onto a wide road overlooking a broad valley, and, keeping the long mané wall on the right, we entered into Hobgoblinland at Lamayuru.

Do not imagine that I shall actually describe Lamayuru to you, for of course I cannot. You still believe that Gulliver never really made those travels and that Lewis Carroll only wrote fairy tales to amuse a child, because he spoke in a language that the world understands—the make-believe. But I know that I followed the White Rabbit who was saying to himself: "Oh my ears and whiskers how late it's getting!" And I hurried

my white pony through quaint streets that were
lined with chortens and manés and ran then off
into narrow courtyards where door jambs were
painted red, and roof-tops piled high with lucerne,
and with hundreds of slender swaying poles tipped
with yaks' tails from which fluttered tattered flags
stamped with invocations and prayers. Sometimes square flags were strung on a cord and ran
all around the roof like a row of handkerchiefs
hung out to dry.

Built up like a pack of cards against a sandstone
cliff rent with great fissures stood a lamasery—a
haphazard group of buildings that seemed to scat-
ter at any angle. Cave eyes looked down from the
vertical fissures as if the habitation ran down into
the bowels of the earth. Such a fantastic tumbled
affair belonged nowhere in any world I had known
and that made me wonder with Alice what Latitude
and Longitude I'd got to.

I could hardly wait to discard the dust of the
road before climbing the heights to see the lamasery
from the inside. It was a fairly easy walk up a winding road that led into a courtyard where the doorways were painted strangely, red predominating.
Red-robed lamas stood around. One of them came
forward questioning: "Who are you?"

I properly replied: "I—I hardly know, sir, just
at present—at least I know who I *was* when I

THE LONELY ROAD.

FOR HOURS THROUGH THE DESERT IN BURNING HEAT.

I COULD SEE THE LARGE NINE-STORIED PALACE TOWERING ABOVE THE TREES.

THERE WAS THE ROW OF PENCIL POPLARS SO OFTEN DESCRIBED.

got up this morning, but I think I must have changed several times since then."

"What do you mean by that? Explain yourself," the lama demanded.

I meekly answered: "I can't explain myself I'm afraid sir, because I'm not myself, you see."

All this being in Ladakhi on his part and English on mine we did not understand each other's speech, but the conversation seemed according to Hoyle or rather according to Alice. And as if satisfied with my lack of identity the lama ushered me into a semi-dark hall where the masks for the Devil Dances are kept, a few of them hanging from gaily decorated columns. The walls were exquisitely painted with allegorical Buddhist stories and although the lama did not even know the date of its execution, so old it was, the colors were as fresh as though recently applied, and in a state of perfect preservation. In the chapel hung many painted banners that take the place of our holy pictures and are so carefully guarded that there is no chance of ever purchasing one from a lamasery, the ones sold being from private collections.

Before the altar were silver tea cups of the proverbial Tibetan type with saucer on a long stem, china cups and lids of silver. There were open bowls of small flowers, holy water pitchers, and perpetual lights fed with butter. In one chapel stood a huge painted statue of Avalokita, most powerful of Buddhas and the one from whom the Delai Lama claims to be reincarnated. The eleven heads here represented denote the agony over the sad state of humanity that rent them asunder; they are arranged cone-like, one upon the other, the forward-looking ones with kindly aspect, the left ones frowning angrily at the sins of men, and those facing right smiling happily over our good deeds. A thousand hands had Avalokita also, spread out into a six-tiered halo back of him, symbols of power, stretched out to save the sinking souls of men. And on these hands are eyes—multitudes of eyes —that look in every direction—the all-seeing!

The monastery is impressive but on leaving the chapel we emerged onto a roof from whence we viewed the mountains and the topsy-turvy town below, looking for all the world like a child's house of blocks that had been knocked down and not put up again. All the solemnity vanished and I felt that I was looking at the stage setting of a comedy.

The dak bungalow at Lamayuru was small but comfortable. I pulled my charpoy out onto the porch and watched the shadows trail off into the night—a soundless night but for the music that seemed to weave itself into the path of a faint moon and set the moonbeams dancing to its mystic measures:

"Harp of the North, farewell! The hills grow dark,
On purple peaks a deeper shade descending;
In twilight copse the glow-worm lights her spark,
The deer, half-seen, are to the covert wending.

. . . .

Thy numbers sweet with nature's vespers blending,

. . . .

Receding now, the dying numbers ring
Fainter and fainter down the rugged dell,
And now the mountain breezes scarcely bring
A wandering witch-note of the distant spell—
And now, 'tis silent all! Enchantress, fare thee well!"

CHAPTER XI

DOWN INTO THE DEEPEST GORGE IN THE WORLD

FROM Lamayuru the road leads on to ever greater interest and enchantment. We started with the first streaks of dawn along a path high on a cliff which rose like a series of turrets out of an unfathomable gorge . . . the deepest in the whole world, it is said. The road ran down into it just as the sun arose upon the world that we were leaving. The coming of a new day to wild, lonely stretches near the Roof of the World is an impressive thing, especially if your path leads down from it into semi darkness.

Down, down, down, the path ran zigzag into the bowels of the earth, terrifying gulfs below holding impenetrable gloom except where a single long thin rock, like Cleopatra's needle, points its white finger into the sky. Margot quoted:

"Upon the utmost verge of a high bank,
By craggy rocks environed round, we came,
Where woes beneath, more cruel yet, were stow'd."

146

Yes, surely Dante's seventh circle lay below! The road dropped two thousand feet among rock cliffs, black even in the growing day, then red where the path opened on to the bed of a stream that had to be forded many times. Just here it was wider and there was not that feeling of doom that seemed to travel with us for most of the way through the Lamayuru Gorge . . .

I got tired of crossing the stream on horseback, never knowing what the pony might be stepping into, what holes might lurk where it eddied about the rocks. So I dismounted and made my way along the right bank, once rounding an overhanging boulder by clinging with feet and hands to its crevices. Then, thinking the distance not too great, I jumped from one high stone to the path on the other side, and landed in the water instead . . . on my feet luckily, which soon dried out in the heat that was becoming more and more intense.

It was like being shut in a hot-box down there as the gorge narrowed, the path ascending for some distance along the narrowest of rock cuttings, uneven ledges with cliffs running straight up beside them and dropping sheer down to the river; not precipices these but khuds, indeed. I hoped that my pony would not slip, but wondered why he did not, as he picked his way over rocks along the extreme edge of a path for miles and

miles. I had taken him on fresh at dawn. I had
not yet learned his ways, and here the path was
too narrow to permit of dismounting. Sometimes rounding sharp corners it seemed to lead off
into space; I never knew whether beyond it would
drop sharply down over rocks, mount over shale,
or continue a mere foothold on this terrifying and
beautiful way to Leh . . .

Rock shelves, rock shelves, and then more rock
shelves . . . would they never end? And yet they
were so beautiful, the colours now flaming skyward
like blue and purple and red chimneys, fiery hot
too with the sun reflecting from them. And such
sublime vistas! Such lights on far off peaks
where a bend of the road opened a wider view, the
shale rock along the path standing up like the blue
and green pages of a book of fairy tales. Then
down again over more shale, and onto a wide
plain . . . a rocky hot plateau. To ease taut
muscles I dismounted and bruised my feet climbing over stones, stubbed my toes and plodded endless stretches of level ground. Above me crevices
in the rock embankments hung like suspended caves
high above the road.

Just there, flung across the wide river Indus
which ran some fifty feet below the road, was a
fine suspension bridge. At this point was built
the first bridge that ever crossed the Indus River

A LONG MANÉ WALL RAN THROUGH THE DESERT WITH CHORTENS
AT BOTH ENDS.

THE TOWN BAND TURNED OUT WITH ITS KETTLEDRUMS.

CIRCUMAMBULATING A SACRED OBJECT TO GAIN MERIT.

THE VAST EXPANSE OF DESERT.

and they tell that inscriptions cut in the rock near-by show Brahmi characters which indicate that it must have dated from 200 B.C. A curse was placed upon any who might seek to destroy it . . . this by King Naglug who built Bragnag castle to protect it. The curse runs thus:

> "Whoever thinks evil of it in his heart
> Let his heart rot!
> Whoever stretches his hand toward it
> Let his hand be cut off!
> Whoever harms it with his eye
> May his eye become blind!
> Whoever does any harm to the bridge
> May that creature be born in Hell!"

Thus warned to respect it, we crossed the bridge, wound up through a chorten gate, by mané walls and along narrow lanes flanked by mud houses. Was it to be Lilliput or Brobding-nag this time? We were certainly in the year of the Earth Serpent, that much was clear, and I was surprised and disappointed to find just the usual rest house sprawling amidst wild honey-suckle vines facing an olive-green cliff of shale that fell in one simple sweep from the tip to where it dropped its toe in the Indus.

Khalatsi, which is about eleven miles from Lamayuru, is only a hundred feet lower, yet it seemed to be cooler. This is the land of the Aryan Dards who kept alive the game of polo after the Persians had ceased to play it. There seemed to be an enterprising air about the place and we decided to halt a day hoping to meet Dr. and Mrs. Kuenick of the Moravian Mission who have done such noble work among the natives of Ladakh. Khalatsi, small though it be, is famous as the place where Dr. Marx the philosopher lived and worked and where Dr. Francke wrote his history of the country.

Unfortunately the Kuenicks were off in the mountains; it was not until the return journey in September that I met them; but there was a lazy day of rest ahead when needle and thread were brought out for much needed mending, and laundry work accomplished, and the necessary repacking of odds and ends in yakdans to say nothing of the writing which always had to be done at the end of every stage lest new sights might obliterate the impressions of a day.

Sandy trailed the hills . . . a gun over his shoulder. Margot and I wandered down to the post office, the last one on the road to Leh, and watched the postman weigh my films. He wore long turquoise earrings and a handsome chain of carnelian and turquoise and spoke excellent English.

We took pictures in the village lanes and out in the field where groups of men and women were having tea together. We were met everywhere with smiles and greetings:

"Zhu-le."

In Khalatsi is the first of the Praying Wheels seen along the route. Their origin has led to much discussion and to fascinating literature. In that interesting book: "The Buddhist Praying Wheel," William Simpson says that as a machine that can be turned by hand the wheel is peculiar to Tibet and Mongolia from whence it found its way into China and Japan, but that in Indian Art it is a symbol, probably a symbol of The Law as Buddha is so frequently represented as Turning the Wheel of the Law. The history of this symbol involves the whole ritual of circular movement including circumambulation and the passing of sacred things and persons keeping the right hand towards them as directed by the Code of Manu. It is recognized to be a solar symbolism of the endless Cycle of Life. The cults and traditions of the ancient peoples of Europe refer to it and the subject, followed from reference to reference, leads one through pages of enchantment in Frazer's "Golden Bough," and Havelock Ellis' "Dance of Life," to references to the Deisul among the Celts. This last was practised down almost to our day in the Highlands of Scotland where moving round in the course of the sun was supposed to bring good luck.

But at Khalatsi I was content just to gain merit by turning the prayer wheel in the street.

CHAPTER XII

AN EASY STAGE. A HARDER ONE. AND A
VISION OF PAST GLORY

WE had only eight miles to go from Khalatsi to Nurla, the next stage. There were mountains of blue and pink and green on each hand and even the shale and sand we trod upon was coloured likewise as the road wound in and out and up and down. There was one sharp descent along a rocky path; a river to ford; beyond, a sharp upward climb along a cutting and out on a wider road where I rubbed my eyes to see if I was awake or merely dreaming. For all about were mountains of robin's egg blue and Egyptian red washed with shades of grey and running up to crags of salmon pink. The road followed along the Indus, so narrow in places that I prayed that I might not meet an oncoming caravan. Here my shoe box with all the cleaning materials for the road slipped from the back of a pack pony and slid down into the river, impossible to retrieve.

My new pony, taken on at Lamayuru and ridden through the gorge, developed a weakness in his hind legs; my second girth buckle broke, and I now rode with a handwoven rope made of yak's hair tied around the saddle to keep it on, and with no breast strap, this having again lost itself among the luggage. The crupper had become a daily wonder; sometimes a rope, sometimes a rag, but enough to hold on to as I descended too steep paths. But whatever else might be lacking in the equipment neither my ponies nor my pony men ever lacked scapulars tied around their necks. . . .

At a point where the mountains parted to let a third peak share the landscape, the sky line of one of them was outlined by twenty-three "sharpoo" plainly counted against the sky . . . a lovely sight. A little farther on the path in front of me was completely washed out, the Indus coursing from cliff to cliff. What could be done? Was the entire road along the embankment washed away to the level of the river bed? Or had the river risen barely enough to cover it leaving a solid path to cross on if one kept close beside the cliff where the road had once been? It looked like one broad stream, as if there had never been a road along there and one could not gauge the depth of the river, though the road could be seen continuing up a shale embankment some distance beyond the break. Margot and Sandy climbed across on the rocks.

My pony tested the road gingerly, a slow step at

a time. If it did not drop suddenly away in front of him all would be well, and to stick on his back seemed to be the surest way of getting across; as long as he touched solid ground the crossing was possible though at the risk of a good wetting. So we followed slowly along beside the over-hanging cliff. My feet were not above the ankles in the water and I had learned from experience that they would dry out quickly in the hot sun. And it was so hot! My face was blistered and sore by the time I reached Nurla at eight o'clock after only two and a half hours on the road. . . .

"You poor little thing," Margot cried when I arrived exhausted and literally fell into the nearest chair.

"Why do people always call me 'little,'" I protested. "I'm as tall as you are . . . five feet six . . ."

"You look as if a puff of wind would blow you away nevertheless. I shall take charge of you. Sandy, fix a whiskey and soda. Call Ali for hot water. Your bedding roll is already undone . . . We've been here an hour. I'll put you to bed."

They would not let me get up for lunch though rest soon restored me. The table was spread beside my cot. We were all in pajamas. Formalities do not last long on a trip like that. Camp meant relaxation. Pajamas spelled comfort. Bad

enough the restrictions of riding breeches and belts
on the road.

Somehow the dak bungalow at Nurla got turned
around. Of course it would out there where everything was topsy-turvy. Instead of facing the bluff,
which rose about two hundred feet above the river,
it sociably hugged the lane that ran between it and
the serai where all the natives of the countryside
came in turns to watch these queer travellers. They
did not find us a bit more interesting than we found
them. All of them wore rings and earrings of
turquoise and bracelets of silver. Their felt boots
had soles of sheepskin or goatskin with the upper
part wide and embroidered in many colours over the
toes. All were filthy, cheerful and kind. They stood
in rows close to the porch, most of them spinning,
with wooden spindles twirling while they unwound
the tufts of grey and black wool carried under their
arms, and some of them spun hand prayer wheels.

We mounted to the roof beyond the serai and
there in a low dark room we found an old blind
Buddhist nun crooning to herself and turning her
prayer wheel as she sat before the fire: "Om mané
padme hum!" While the Western world is absorbed with material progress the East is absorbed
in prayer.

At Nurla one is still forty-five miles from Leh.
Jackals barked through the night and thunder

LIKE A BIRD CAGE THE SQUARE BUILDING HANGS ON THE VERY EDGE OF A
CLIFF—THE RED GOMPA ON NAMGYALT HILL.

THE WRITER IN MESPOT TOPI, SUN SHIELD
AND DARK GLASSES.

THE SKUSHOK OF HEMIS SIGNED AND STAMPED THIS PICTURE OF HIMSELF
FOR THE AUTHOR.

growled among the mountains, and the men were unusually still in the cookhouse alongside the dak bungalow.

A bad road runs beyond Nurla to Saspul, the next stage . . . the whole of it a desert route with but two little baghs. We left Nurla at four in the morning, following down a khud at dawn after rounding chortens and manis. The road wound up and down until we struck sheer up the face of a cliff at zigzag, so steep a climb that I almost pulled my pony over backwards, and his saddle slipped. For both our sakes I had to dismount and make my own way up over the boulders, panting as did the ponies with the exertion in that altitude.

This was the steepest climb of the whole route and I wondered how the pack ponies would ever make it under their cumbersome loads of about a hundred and sixty pounds each. They fell time and again to their knees as they were pushed and pulled up by the pony men. It is because of such bits as this that it is wise to secure at least one pony man to every two ponies, one to each if possible.

This rock ladder at last gave on to a wider space from whence the descent immediately began on the other side. Half way up I managed to get the camera coolie to come to me in time to take a brief moving picture of the mounting pack ponies, but these most interesting sights usually occurred so unexpectedly that I was not prepared or I might be on a narrow rock ledge perched at such precarious angle that picture taking was impossible.

Over boulders and shale the road ran then. Sometimes it mounted narrow winding rock ledges or crossed flimsy bridges with sheer cliffs rising all about, sometimes headed down zigzag where it seemed as if one's next step must be over the edge, so sharp the turns for four legs to make. The pony edged around them while again I envied Margot and Sandy who were strong enough to make the trip on foot. I wanted to be closer to the ground and occasionally to touch that wall on the inner side. . . .

Copper, green, blue and saffron . . . every possible hue those mountains had, patterned in strange swirls across shale cliffs as if a giant brush had swept across them. There, in just the proper setting, rode a man perched high on the rugs across his saddle, rugs of blue and yellow with a huge copper bowl tied on behind, glinting in the sunlight.

A low broad pass followed the Indus which broadens towards Saspul and grows to immense width as it tracks across the desert from Leh, the cradle of its birth being, it is said, somewhere in the vicinity of sacred Mount Méru where is also the location of the Buddhist Heaven. . . .

The dak bungalow at Saspul, fourteen and a half miles from the last stage, is the only two-storied one along the road.   It is spacious and comfortable with an upper porch and wide compound set in the cool shade of green willows.   Below in the court-yard our men were soon at work building the fire, always the first act on entering camp or compound, for the sahibs must bathe forthwith and also eat. Kadera was given small sums whenever necessary to purchase supplies of wood, kerosene, milk and cooking butter, which he clarified, also eggs and chickens when these were obtainable.   Sandy, who was running the bandobast, guarded the stores carefully.   We arrived at Leh with most of the sup-plies we had taken out.   This shows how well one can do on the journey with far less than we carried, for at this point we still had twenty-one pack ponies.   But the length of our stay in Leh was in-definite and the journey back had been planned for a different route so it was wise to husband the stores though it made for a monotonous fare.

At five the next morning we left Saspul and turned away from the Indus River.   The road rose over a steep hill to the Rong Là. This is only a mule path which carries one for hours through the desert in such burning heat that time and again I felt dizzy and sick.   I tried to jog myself into a jocose mood by reciting to myself:

"The Walrus and the Carpenter
Were walking close at hand,
They wept like anything to see
Such quantities of sand:
'If this were only cleared away,'
They said, 'It would be grand'."

It was useless. I felt wretchedly.

The mountains were now green on one side of
the path and red on the other and opened out upon
a wide desert. Here and there little piles of stones
were set up. Lhatos these, offerings of lonely herds-
men, sometimes perched on high points of rock
fluttering a prayer flag from the apex. Turning
down a hill we saw the path strewn thick with low-
growing yellow flowers. On beyond lay Bazgo,
the most picturesque of all the towns of the road,
a ruined town where flowers and purple sage sprout
through the rock walls and wheat grows at the
level of one's head along the sunken road.

There are flowers everywhere sprouting through
cracks and crannies, but somehow they seemed like
the smiles behind which misery barricades itself,
or the hand with which a page is shielded that pry-
ing eyes looking over one's shoulder may not read
what is recorded there. For Bazgo had had its
Springtime long ago, and the jumble of its red sandstone dwellings, that seem to shrink against the red
cliff as if to ask for obscurity, is beautiful now

like the face of a person who has lived intensely
and in declining years has taken on an expression
of aloofness that shadows memories . . . the mystery of distance travelled that some eyes reflect.

The crazy, tumbled, half-ruined dwellings look
out over a wide plateau that more than once has
resounded to the clash of armour, for here were
fought battles, where lances gleamed, red-tufted,
in the sun; where arrows and stone slings found
the vulnerable spot of the enemy. The palace at
Bazgo withstood a three year siege when Mongols
invaded Ladakh. Then the King implored the help
of the Emperor of India, Shah Jehan, who sent a
huge army and exacted heavy pay for his assistance, the adoption of Islam by the country being
part of the tribute. Shah Jehan was the tenth in
direct descent from Tamerlane and was called the
"King of the World.". . .

Margot and Sandy had caught up with me, but
I did not stop with them to eat in Bazgo. I pushed
on to Niemu which in the rarified air looked so
close . . . a green oasis in a desert of desolation.
It seemed to be only a half hour's march away, but
eluded me hour after hour until I began to wonder
if I had really seen Niemu or just a mirage. At
last, exhausted from the heat, face blistered from
the burning desert sun, and hair like straw, I
stretched weary limbs in a comfortable dak bun-

galow. Even twenty days of trekking had not hardened muscles that a lifetime had never put to use.
I was so sick all through the night at Niemu that
I longed to wait over a day there but was able to
resume the journey at dawn. . . .

The caravan was some time getting in that
afternoon, and a charpoy with wide braids instead
of springs is more comfortable than an iron bed;
one rests quite comfortably on them until one's
bedding roll arrives with greater comforts. At
Niemu there were sand flies, and feet, blistered from
the gravel that seeped in between chaplie straps,
had to be doctored in spite of the precaution I had
taken of rubbing them before starting with car-
bolated vaseline. Also I had drunk all the water
in my canteen along the road where no water was
to be found, and I had to stand an aching thirst
until the ponies came in and water could be boiled
for drinking. It seemed as though I could never
take enough of it along for the desert stages and I
strongly suspected that Happy, who carried my
canteen, had helped himself out of it, so short a
time had it lasted.

CHAPTER XIII

INTO THE PROMISED LAND

It was August fifth and the last stage of the journey that would bring us into Leh. We left Niemu at a quarter to five, the ponies a sorry lot. Although they had been called for in the morning of the day before they were not brought in until just before dawn, and this only after a house to house canvas by Sandy and Kadera during the night. Sandy's temper was unmentionable next morning. There was confusion in getting started. The ponies reared and threw off their packs, and the black beast that I was to ride seemed more of an uncertain quantity than I liked to contemplate. At least there were no khuds ahead, only desert stretches, and I fancied that if I were to be thrown it would be on soft sand.

I soon found however that the entire desert was covered with small stones which made going difficult as the pony was in danger of turning his foot on the hidden ones. Patches of sage varied the monotony somewhat, but though the mountains about were snow-capped, they sent down no cooling

163

breeze and it was a weary stretch in grilling heat. I tried walking and riding alternately, but it was difficult going in sandals that did not fit and offered little protection from gravel that seeped through between the straps. The hills ran down in sweeps of olive-green rock, shaded into brick red, and between their gaps showed distant snow ranges. The whole countryside seemed to have an air of watchfulness, of aloofness. . . .

Sandy had passed on ahead of me. Margot was behind.

We passed Spitug; its monastery, five hundred years old and spreading across grey rock that rose beside the Indus, was less imposing than the one at Lamayuru and we did not halt there. From Spitug the road mounted steadily one thousand feet in four miles, but the grade was scarcely noticeable; the desert sands were thickly strewn with partly concealed rocks, making bad going on foot or horseback. . . .

"Jelde! Jelde!" "Hurry up!"

The sun was blistering hot in the desert waste. But my Ladakhi pony heeded not and carefully picked his way among the rocks, his weak hind foot occasionally giving way under him so that I could not relax my vigilance. Leh, referred to by its inhabitants always as Ladakh, was a green illusion in the distance, seeming so near that a few minutes ride would reach it, but ever keeping afar off.

Long before arriving at its gate I could see the large nine-storied palace towering above the trees. A long mané wall ran through the desert with chortens at both ends. Finally the road turned in through a walled-in lane, mounted some stone steps and led across the high sill of a huge wooden door into the Bazaar of Leh.

There was the row of pencil poplars so often described; the quaint shops; the mosque at the far end of the wide dirt street; but where was the motley throng crowding the main thoroughfare? There should have been slit-eyed Mongolians, fair-skinned Yarkandis with high felt boots and fur caps, Tajiks from Bokhara and Russian Turkestan, Persians and Arabs and Chinese. . . . They were absent. Yet there four roads meet to link the trade that comes down over the Khardong Pass from Central Asia and Yarkand, from Tibet and China, and two of them from down India, the one running via Kulu and Lahoul to Simla and the other that we had come by from Kashmir.

It was eleven o'clock as I rode in. The streets were almost deserted. Lean years had come to Leh; floods had kept the caravans away. A turn of the road brought a group of women into view, all of them decked in their gay peyraks, turquoise-studded, and with capes of goatskin about their shoulders and tight fitting trousers cut so long that they wrinkled up. They were marketing, and baskets of grain and apricots were stacked beside the road. And, wonder of wonders! There were little dark children playing hop-scotch just as I used to do at school in America. I turned into a narrow lane walled in between houses of sun-dried brick, a stream running down one side, then into the wide shady compound of the dak bungalow.

The pack ponies did not get in until two o'clock . . . a long wait. But there were comfortable chairs and I rested a bit and shook off some of the dust of travel before going with Sandy, who had been in some time, to make the customary visit of courtesy on the British Joint Commissioner. The Residency adjoins the rest house compound, a two-storied white building with life-sized Chinese figures painted on each side of the main entrance. It is surrounded by a shady garden where one has a view over the snow-covered Zanskar range across the Indus River. Mount Sacrifice at twenty thousand feet was plainly visible.

Captain and Mrs. Falconer returned our call the same evening and invited us to dinner next day. They sent over magazines and newspapers and a tray full of fresh vegetables and showed never-failing hospitality during the long stay in Leh.

AN OLD CHORTEN, LEH.

That afternoon I went also to see Colonel and Mrs. Berry who had been so kind to me in Kashmir. They occupied a wee bungalow in the Mission compound just below the dak bungalow and it was good to see familiar faces in that far away place. Next day the Moravian Bishop came to see us. Thus we had met the entire white population of Leh.

Colonel Berry secured me a Ladakhi bearer which was a stroke of luck as there seemed to be no men seeking positions of that kind in Leh. This one could not speak or understand English, but he proved to be as trustworthy as he looked and I kept him with me all summer, sign language being our means of communication. Tall and thin was Gulam, with Mongolian features, his eyes very keen, his air alert and gestures quick. Gulam means slave. He was all of that to me. . . .

At last we were in Leh about which so many dreams had centred! We had arrived without mishap, the "ambulance" even untouched. This was the far away and mysterious place . . . a disappointment at first. There seemed to be little to do; the shops held nothing of special interest; even the few curio shops which depend on the caravans to supply them, held little to attract me. I succeeded in finding two huge chang (fermented barley water) jugs bound in metal, and the Chinese

saddle rugs to go with a saddle that was ridden
by a man in the one polo match that was staged
during our visit in Leh. I traced him through
a merchant in town and found him most willing
to part with it for what he thought an enormous
sum. Later I was offered the tea churn of the
Queen of Ladakh and was allowed to purchase a
beautiful rice bowl from the kitchen of the leading
merchant of the town who had got it in Lhasa.
These were my sole acquisitions in Leh where even
cigarettes and canned goods are scarce and the
paper to wrap purchases in altogether lacking; and
of course there is no such thing as a newspaper
there to use instead of wrapping paper.

The people of Leh are friendly; their eyes are
full of merry things that make you think of dancing and laughter, and they greet you always with
a smile. Their features are Mongolian and you
would say that they are dark-skinned until you saw
the Christian women and children who are washed;
they look fair with lovely rosy cheeks. Christians
number about a hundred and the women have discarded the peyrak and hair braided in many tiny
plaits joined at the end with a tassel, for the stove-
pipe hat of brocade with pointed ear flaps which
is worn also by the men, and which is far less attractive than the turquoise headdress. . . .

We started housekeeping in style in the six-room

bungalow. No need to hoard stores now. Enough was set aside for the return journey.

"Good Lord! Here's actually a bottle of Marnier." Sandy was opening box number eight.

"Let's ask the Falconers to dinner!"

Our centerpiece was waiting by the roadside to be picked. We borrowed plates from the Residency and the Falconers came over to eat their own lettuce.

Everyone in Leh seemed to be waiting for a caravan which never arrived. Meantime the Wazir came and a polo match was held in his honour when the town band turned out with its kettledrums, trumpets and clarionets. The game took place in a side street, Sandy joining in a bit bewildered by the fact that his mount could not be induced to approach the ball. It is Ladakhi humour to provide the visitor with a trick horse and Sandy was lucky that his did not dash for the nearest wall. Polo in Leh has little resemblance to the game as we know it at home.

CHAPTER XIV

LEH

It never rains in Leh, but it is terribly hot in the sun in spite of the altitude of 11,500 feet. We took sightseeing leisurely . . . but did not neglect it.

Leh has two immense statues of Chamba or Maitreya, the Buddha who is to come, both of them seated figures with legs hanging down as Chamba is always pictured, and each of them is so tall that its shoulders touched the ceiling of the chapel and had its head confined in a second story building. One of them was in a gompa up one of the dark lanes in Leh, another in a lamasery perched high on Namgyalt hill overlooking the town. To this I climbed one day with Mrs. Berry along a narrow path, steep up a sandy embankment, slipping back at every step in spite of a walking stick. Like a bird cage the square building hangs on the very edge of a cliff, the road winding up to it very steep near the top with a sheer drop of a thousand feet at one side. The sun was blistering hot and it was a fatiguing climb in such altitude.

I entered the little building much as I would wind through a maze. The path led up and round three sides of it and landed me on a narrow rail-less plank balcony that had to be traversed clear around the four sides of the building at its second story before I reached the entrance. It was nerve-racking business! The platform hung sheer over the cliff. I wanted to say that I would not attempt it; but I wanted still more to see Chamba and the only way that I could do so was to make the circuit of the building on that gallery of planks hung seemingly in space. Also I felt a bit ashamed of my cowardice when I saw Mrs. Berry advance with-out a tremor. At least it was a comfort to touch a wall with my left hand as I crept along. It was horrid turning the corners, just air beyond and the drop of a thousand feet. How glad I was to step over the high sill and see eye to eye with Chamba! One stands on a level with the chin. The lack of modelling and the immense size of the statue give the effect of peace and power, not unlike the im-pression one has on seeing the Colossus of Rameses at Memphis. There is aloofness and serenity in the Buddha's face.

Rounding the ledge again one enters the lower chamber where at the feet of the statue are the usual offerings of stemless flowers and perpetual lights floating in ghee or butter. A lama was in attendance who was grateful for our small offering.

It was delightful to go about with Mrs. Berry, who travels sympathetically and was devoid of that scorn that some people affect for the religious symbols that they do not venerate themselves. The world has grown accustomed to seeing Catholics crown their miraculous statues with great ceremony; or kiss the toe of Saint Peter's statue in the Basilica at Rome. People in the Philippines see the little black statue of the Infant Jesus . . . the Santo Niño of Cebu, clothed in brocades studded with precious stones, or the devout burn candles by the thousands before some miraculous shrine. These things are familiar. But when primitive people picture their deity representative of the power, vengeance, terror or infinite peace as they conceive them, some people are prone to ridicule. What the devil with his pitchfork is to the Christian, to those of other lands are the many arms grasping instruments of torture. I once heard a learned Hindu explain that the various gods worshipped in India were "aspects" of divinity; that God "limited" himself in a million ways to express himself in flowers, perfume, the dashing torrent, the mighty cliffs and the clear pure air . . . all evidences of His omnipresence.

The first month of the year finds hundreds of

pious Buddhists performing the humble practise of circumambulating some sacred object . . . to gain merit. In Benares, the secred city on the Ganges where the Lord Buddha preached, they do it all around the city, which takes six days and is rewarded by the remission of sins. These pious practices are performed in the same spirit as animates the Catholic who seeks to gain indulgences. In Leh they circumambulate the mané walls and even the red gompa on the high hill by moving around the entire hill, sun-wise, keeping the sacred object on the right. We could not be in Leh at the time of this ceremony so Gulam arranged for two Ladakhis to give us a demonstration that we might photograph it. Prone they lay full length in the dust, hands outstretched above their heads as they measured their length on the ground beside a mané wall. Then they arose, walked to the spot where the tip of their fingers had touched and repeated the prostration. But since we must have the proper light to photograph them they could not move sun-wise as is proper. The Tibetan name for the lengthy process seems to fitly describe it. They call it "Kora-la Kyang chang ches pa."

Leh offered many novel sights. Once it was an entertainment by the British Joint Commissioner which lasted all afternoon and evening. School children displayed their prowess in high jumps much the same as they do with us, and after other athletic feats refreshments were served in several tents; one for Hindus, one for Mohamedans, one for Ladakhis, one for native "Personages" and one for Europeans with whom Americans are classed in the East. In the evening there were native dances, a lovely sight in the garden where the lights of torches reflected among the trees. It recalled an entertainment General Pershing had once given in the garden of his home in Zamboanga in the Philippines when he was in command there; there were native dances then too and torchlight.

Once also I visited a poor woman's house . . . the home of the Bishop's servant. We entered a courtyard with high stone walls where a pony was tethered; the house entrance was through a dark hall, but stairs led up to an open roof from where one looked over the town and the vast expanse of desert. The most important room was the kitchen where rafters were blackened but where everything else was immaculately clean, pots shining, the low tea table set with glistening tea pots. There were also pictures of Christ . . . (the servant was a Christian) and photographs of Queen Mary and King George which she displayed with pride. . . .

CHAPTER XV

HEMIS AND THE DEVIL DANCES

WE left Leh early in the morning of August 11th for a trip to the famous lamasery of Hemis, which next to the Potala in Lhasa is the most famous of all those in the land of Greater Tibet of which Ladakh once was part. It lies twenty-three miles to the south and east of Leh across the Indus River.

Floods had prevented our crossing earlier. For many days they had held caravans waiting on banks where bridges had been washed away. It had looked for a time as if we should be forced to abandon the trip. Then word was brought in that a native had succeeded in fording the Indus just below Leh, and we decided to try the crossing, taking with us only the necessary tents and supplies.

Bishop Peter had taken me to call on the Skushok of Hemis when he was in Leh where he had come to greet the Wazir representing the Maharajah of Kashmir. We had passed through the entrance of a small square building into a dark hall where we made our way over slippery stones, up an

175

equally slippery stone stairway to a ladder at the head of which a courteous lama greeted us and ushered us into the presence of the "skushok." The latter had come forward and greeted us in a most friendly way, taking our hands in turn between both of his and motioning us to be seated where two chairs were drawn up beside the low cushioned seat on which he sank.

A low stand in front of him held the usual porcelain tea cup in its long-stemmed silver saucer and cover tipped with carnelian, a bowl of apricots, another of flowers cropped off at the head. Apricots and tea were offered to us but I, having heard something about the indigestibility of butter-tea such as is exclusively drunk in these parts, declined on the plea that I had just finished my lunch.

The walls were hung with a few scroll paintings but held nothing else of great interest. The conversation, translated by the Bishop, expressed great interest in America, chiefly in our tall buildings and the fact that a woman should travel so far from home alone. I spoke of my desire to visit Hemis and to see the Devil Dances there, and he cordially invited me to do so, offering me his own bungalow there or his tents.

The skushok pulled out a small notebook from the folds of his ample robe and asked me to write my name and address in it. He told me that every facility would be afforded me for seeing the monastery and taking photographs of Hemis.

It had been difficult to secure horses, the few available ones being either wretched specimens or fractious animals such as I could not ride. But the necessary number had been at last assembled and we started out, I on this occasion in advance of the others, and on the sorriest mount I had yet ridden.

The Indus, which is very wide at this point, rises considerably by seven in the morning and we were warned to attempt the crossing only before that hour. So it was at dawn that we set out from Leh.

Down a gorge, along mané walls and chortens, and then over a monotonous stretch of stony desert the path led; there I thought that because it was flat and seemingly safe from accident I might relax the eternal vigilance that was so nerve-racking along much of the road. All of a sudden I found myself being hurled through the air over the horse's head. But fortunately I struck the brim of my topi which saved my head from worse than a severe jolt, while my right knee hit a hidden rock giving me somewhat the sensation of a battlefield.

After some dizzy moments I tried to stand up and eventually, leaning on the shoulder of my bearer, I hobbled along until the stiffness wore off while the pony man helped the poor little beast to his feet. It had turned a weak hind foot on a stone and fallen flat; a great welt was on its side where it also had struck a rock.

Watching it later being led ahead of me I saw that at each step the foot turned over on the side. It was a long way to hobble to the river but I preferred that to getting on its back again and was miserable when later I had to ride it across the torrent.

It was very hot in the desert even at the early hour and my knee was swelling painfully and so fast that the one-time very loose breeches bound too tightly. I was none too happy starting for Hemis that August day.

I reached the river bank. The bridge was washed out for many yards, a torrent of water hurling itself high through the aperture. I sat down on a rock near by feeling dizzy and sick, my head swimming. Sandy came up with Margot. I followed them, along the bridge to the edge of the break. Sandy was talking to a native who was then engaged to wade across ahead of us.

It was bad going. The coolie had his clothes rolled high under his arm pits; he found the shallowest parts which actually made two crossings, a sand bank breaking the depth part way. The swirling waters coming with great force through the break in the bridge just behind and to the left made my horse press to the right; I leaned toward the left thinking to counterbalance this. Everything swam before my eyes, uncertain as I was of the direction I was following, but certain that if I fell off I should be swept down stream. I thought all the while of my pony's weak hind foot and the rocky bottom.

My pony man called "Kabardar! Kabardar!" Sandy called to me: "Sit up straight. You are leaning too much to one side."

My feet dangled in the water; I was dizzy and sure that I was going to fall off whether the saddle turned or not. But at last I was across . . . the pack ponies following.

I had crossed rivers on railless bamboo rafts drawn by a swimming carabao who had a rope run through his nostril for steering gear. I had made landings while waves dashed over the sedan chair in which coolies carried me from row boat to shore. I had been carried ashore on men's backs and had ridden the breakers in rowboats. . . . But I had never crossed water with such a sense of helpless misery as I felt when I forded the wide Indus at flood tide.

Yet Fear is a wonderful emotion. It is living at high speed.

Once across I dismounted. My saddle had slipped to one side. The effort to straighten it and cinch the old girth that had still one of its

buckles left, broke that remaining one and a rope
was tied around it to hold it on.

A bit beyond I changed to my bearer's mount
and made better headway along the most weari-
some and monotonous desert stretch of the whole
journey and in heat so great that twice I had to
stop in baghs and rest until the dizziness passed.
I thought the journey would never end; just on
and on through sand, hour after hour, my knee
painful and stiff bent in the saddle, but the sand
scorching through my hobnailed boots when I tried
to walk. Endless desert rolled up even into the
hills which were sandy and colourless, a few baghs
along the road offering momentary resting places.
In one we rested and had refreshments and slept
for awhile under tamarisk trees, then had to push
on again through the grilling heat of early afternoon. . . .

The route finally turned from the Indus River
and mounted a ravine to the right. There was no
regular path. Twilight was coming. It was a
lonely spot. Margot and I were alone. We both
rode wretched horses. Sandy was far on ahead.
At last we came to mané walls and chortens leading up to the ravine. A lama in long red robe and
peaked red hat, belonging to the red sect of Hemis,
pointed the direction to a gateway that entered a
bagh set high above the road. . . . There was our

LAMASERY OF HEMIS.

DEVIL DANCERS OF HEMIS.

LAMASERY OF HEMIS.

DEVIL DANCERS OF HEMIS.

camp, the pack ponies having gone on ahead with Sandy.

There was a call to make on Bishop Peter of Leh who had preceded us and had arranged the visit for us and who was camped somewhere in the same bagh. He was to fix the hour for our visit to the monastery and our visit to the skushok next day before he returned to Leh. We had tea with him in his tent; I was then glad to seek my cot and let Margot and Sandy do the honours of the bandobast when he came that same evening to dine with us. I had my repast in bed, wondering whether I should be able to walk at all next day. It was so still in the growing twilight that I fell asleep.

I was awakened by a clarion call that rumbled like thunder among the mountains, its last echo scarcely stilled before it broke out again with increasing volume. I rubbed my eyes, wondering, then I remembered that we were in Hemis on a visit to the skushok.

The last note died away . . . there was unutterable silence, my ears straining to catch a lingering vibration. Then came the reeds like sobs shuddering through the twilight stillness, these in turn silenced by a long blast from conch shells and the roll of muffled drums, all dying on the air and pausing before the great shawms again sent out their cry in swelling volume that echoed down the ravine.

How weird! How unearthly! How compelling, this religious service of the lamas that lasts for an hour or more, rising, falling, rising, falling; and never so wonderful as when heard at dusk or when breaking through the silence of the night, the countryside reverberating to the strangely measured, lulling notes.

The flaps of my tent were drawn back. About me was a thick grove of willows inside of a walled garden. Some distance away were the tents of my companions, and farther on, in another break in the thicket, our cook tent with servants gathered over the camp fire near a huge pole tipped with a yak's tail and fluttering tattered flags stamped with Buddhist prayers, all ending with the sentence: "May Buddha's doctrine prosper."

Hemis lies in a narrow ravine, which is the main reason for its having escaped destruction during the invasion of the country by the Dogras. For that reason its vast library, its famous masks and embroidered robes used in the miracle plays are the best in the country. Hemis is also the largest landowner in Ladakh and may be said to be a rich community as riches are counted there. The lamasery is spread out against a stark grey cliff. It is painted white with balconies running across wide windows hung with curtains fringed with gold. The tops of the windows are quaintly fashioned and projecting, an architectural feature of Ladakh.

To reach the lamasery next day we crossed a narrow bridge, mounted along a wide lane that led finally through a massive doorway into a courtyard about fifty feet long by perhaps thirty feet wide. A broad stone stairway to the left led up to the main entrance and prayer room which we were invited to visit. There we saw a large statue of Buddha and an enormous silver chorten set with gold and jewels, tea cups in fringed petticoats and bowls of silver, butter lamps, the dorjé and bell, and bowls of stemless flowers. Above were rafters red painted and beautifully decorated, the colours toned and mellowed with age. Painted banners hung from every wall and rafter, things of exquisite workmanship seen clearly in the light that entered only through the immense doorway. The lamas, a cheerful lot, were laughing merrily as they donned their robes and masks. We were escorted by one of them along the courtyard, up a flight of steps on to a roof and then to a narrow balcony facing the large entrance door. There the skushok welcomed us.

A wild flare of trumpets and drums broke out, and down the wide stairway with measured tread came eight lamas decked in elaborate robes, large masks covering their heads, some representing ghouls, some horned beasts. They swung round

and round the tall pole in the courtyard from which
hung a prayer flag, dancing with revolving motion
sun-wise, in which direction also they moved round
the pole.   They whirled and whirled while I took
motion pictures and still pictures.   And in the lulls
of music they dashed up the steps to reappear
again shortly in other masks, repeating the same
dancing.   This was of course a special feature arranged in my honour and was not altogether like
the Devil Dances that take place once a year in the
monastery and which last for three days and are
really a mystery play.   But it was similar and gave
a good idea of what the big celebration was.

After it was over we visited the monastery itself
and the skushok's own quarters there which were
at that time being redecorated, red the predominating note with elaborate designs on doorways and
rafters.

We passed out of the lamasery by another gate,
down a lane beside the building where a long row
of little prayer wheels were let into the wall. As we
twirled each one in passing, sun-wise to gain merit,
the cylinders revolving set in vibration the many
times printed prayer of praise: "Om mané padme
hum!" . . .

Then we were escorted to a bungalow that was
gay with painted beams and flowers and were
greeted by the skushok who held his pet pekinese

in his arms. Talking with him this time was not so interesting, as the bishop had returned to Leh and we had no interpreter. Sandy had to make himself understood in Urdu which the skushok affects not to know but understands a little. He is interested in postage stamps and has a large collection, and he is interested in mechanical toys, and was engrossed with my motion picture camera with which he took my picture after he had posed in the garden for me to take his. He gave me also a postcard picture of himself which he signed and stamped with his personal seal in red ink, the ink a paste contained in nothing more formidable than a small jar such as you can purchase at any grocer's containing *paté-de-foie-gras*. . . .

The head of the Hemis monastery is of medium height, inclined to stoutness, impassive face of Mongolian type, but with eyes alert. He is entirely unaffected, seemingly unselfconscious and simple in his manner which is a remarkable thing, for his position is very great in the land, second only to that of the Dalai Lama of Lhasa. He is an absolute monarch; he makes laws for others that he need not abide by himself, for he is above evil; no deed of his can be counted against him; he is sought and courted by the great from all lands if they visit this country . . . and he is in the prime of life, having been born in 1883, and believes himself to be what he is popularly stated to be . . . the reincarnation of the founder of Hemis.

When a skushok dies he is believed to reincarnate in some child. All infants born under miraculous portents after his death are eagerly sought throughout the land and subjected to severe tests by a court composed of the chief Tibetan reincarnated lamas and the great lay officials of the state; their parentage is investigated and, like all lamas, they must be free from physical defect.

These infants then have placed before them duplicate collections of the possessions of the recently deceased and the one who recognizes his property is assumed to be his reincarnation. But to assure accuracy they are balloted with prayer and worship over a period of from thirty-one to seventy-one days by many lamas selected for their purity. The names are written on slips of paper which are then rolled in balls of paste and dropped into a golden jug from whence, with unceasing prayer, the name is drawn. The skushok is then left in the care of his mother for eight years when he is turned over to a tutor who fits him for the novitiate. It is easy to picture the tender care and awe of the mother. The skushok knows nothing but absolute submission from those about him, yet there was not a trace of condescension in the bearing of the man before us. Rather I felt an eagerness about him that was restrained by long habit and the dignity of his position.

The theory of reincarnate lamas is said to have originated about the fifteenth century and to have been at first a scheme to secure stability of succession. All of this I learned in that most fascinating book "Lamaism in Tibet," by Waddell. . . .

At five o'clock next morning we left for the return journey. We crossed the Indus near Hemis, this time on a swaying bridge that seemed not to have a long life ahead of it, and trailed through the desert for weary hours. Tikse, with its imposing monastery on a cliff, varied the scenery, then Shea, where we broke the journey by making camp for a night and where a "tamasha" or celebration, was in full swing, the lane beside our camping ground gay with men and women decked in holiday attire. Then we went on to Leh next morning, passing on the way the British Joint Commissioner and Mrs. Falconer who were journeying to make an official call at Hemis.

CHAPTER XVI

RIDING TO THE STARS AT 16,000 FEET

WE had been almost three weeks in Leh and beyond deciding that we would return by the same
route instead of going north over the plains of the
Deo Sai or south via Suru as we had planned, we
had not mentioned our return to Kashmir.

But Sandy's vacation was almost over and I
knew that Margot had planned to join friends in
Gulmarg early in September and there was yet
another trip that I was determined to make before
I returned.

North of Leh rise the greatest mountains in the
world . . . the Karakorum Range, and beyond that
the Mustagh holding the largest glaciers outside
of those in Polar regions. The gateway to this
grandeur is the Khardong Pass which my map
of survey, 1927, gives as 18,142 feet high. It is led
up to by a steep and difficult climb from the Leh
side and runs off into miles of treacherous snow
beds on the other, the path, they say, lined with the
carcasses of animals who tried to cross and failed.
Beyond the Khardong run the Shyok and the

YAKS FROM OVER THE KHARDONG.

ARCHITECTURE IN LEH IS QUAINT.

Nubra Rivers. The path leads to Chinese Turkestan and to Yarkand and Samarkand and is pass-
able only during a few weeks in summer and then
only by the very hardy. But to reach the summit
is the aspiration of some who go to Leh and it was
my ambition. Margot decided not to try it. I
planned to go alone but Sandy would not hear of
it. . . .

Yaks, with their great lungs and their short
sturdy legs, stand both the altitude and the crossing of snow beds with less exertion and danger
than ponies do; they can pull themselves out of
the snow in which ponies flounder helplessly under
loads. There was no way to procure yaks at Leh
and even ponies were difficult to find, but Sandy
managed finally to secure the necessary mounts.
He and I started after tea on August the sixteenth.
We had been advised to break the journey by camping at the foot of the Pass in order to have a fresh
start for the steep pull to the summit. We took
only two pack ponies besides the mounts for ourselves and our bearers, I on a sorry little mare whose
foal followed close at heel annoying her constantly.

After leaving Leh and passing the usual mané
walls and chortens we found that the road, at gradual up grade, ran along sandy embankments between rocky, barren hills, a hard pull for the pony
that halted at every few paces panting painfully

and needing to be urged on constantly. This was fatiguing for me in that altitude especially as the saddle kept slipping back and the stirrup came loose on the steep grades.

It grew dark so fast, shut in between high mountains as we were, that we saw no chance of reaching the foot of the pass while there was still light enough to see the road, and so we decided to camp where we found fairly level ground strewn with rocks and cut up by rivulets which afforded the necessary water for the horses. It was then half past seven. Our bearers soon had a lusty fire going with the wood we had brought along and while dinner was cooking we had time to supervise the arranging of our effects for the night.

A small tent was put up for me but I elected to sleep out in the open and had my canvas cot placed in one small clearing among the rocks while Sandy found another close by, and the men another. It was difficult to find any one spot large enough and level enough that was free from trickling water. Dinner was spread out on a bath towel with dish towels as napkins as we had forgot to bring table linen, and I am sure that no feast ever tasted so good though our ambrosia and nectar were just baked beans, sausages, canned peas, canned butter and tea with canned cream. . . .

Ahead of us were great dark cliffs, shutting off

view of those higher ranges towering up to twenty-
five, twenty-six, twenty-eight thousand feet; and
we think of Mount McKinley as high at 20,300
feet because it is the highest in North America!
Behind us was the sunset tinging with pink the
one peak of snow that rose remote and inaccessible between dark ranges.   The map shows snow
beds there at 18,949 feet.

The stars came out, robbing the bleak landscape
of its loneliness.   The moon climbed high while
the glow of sunset lingered and we did not need
even lantern light for our repast.   We talked little.
Talking is a bit of an effort where the air is light
as lithium.   Explorers at sea level with greater
atmospheric pressure can breathe easier.   High
altitudes do not afford sufficient oxygen, and vital-
ity is lowered; it is even difficult to stand the
weight of the clothing necessary to keep out the
cold.   When describing the spot to others later I
was told that we had reached approximately sixteen thousand feet, which is higher than the pinnacle of Mt. Blanc.   After dinner we thought of
sleep at once, for the start was to be at dawn, and
the climb would be a strenuous one.

But I could not sleep.   I was not even conscious of fatigue just then.   It was for me too
glorious an experience.   I found a boulder near
my cot that offered splendid support for my back

as I sat on the ground absorbing the wonder of the night. Never had I known a moment of absolute quiet during any of the twenty-four hours in the big city where I was at home, and here it was like living a mystery; like being adrift among improbabilities, in Space and Time such as they must have been before creation; or it might be the brink of eternity. Surely there could never be another dawn . . . the night was so vast.

The moon dominated all like an eye of eternal vigilance; as high and as proud as love. Strange that until so recently it should have been called a "dead world."

"When I consider Thy heavens; the work of Thy fingers; the moon and the stars which Thou hast ordained; what is man that Thou art mindful of him?"

Yet it seemed to me that to have been part of His thought at all in the midst of such immensity robbed man of his insignificance.

The camp fire glowed and crackled with the twigs we had brought along. The figures of our men were outlined against the sky, their voices muffled. Doubtless prayers, as always, were on their lips. "There is no God but God." . . . They were all Mohamedans.

What a memory to treasure! The stream trick-

ling down among the rocks. Shadows of haunting
melody and madness flitting in the moonlight, like
those notes of the great shawms of Hemis dying
into muffled echoes, and the sigh of reeds wafted
down the ravine! Up there on such a night the
grasp of one's old world was no stronger than a
basting thread; values were different; one took out
and looked over the things that one had tucked
away in a corner of one's soul: Sorrows . . . always
"mal entrées"; ecstasies that led you to high
heaven; and the things that put your foundations
all awry; the things that after all made your soul
grow to whatever it had become. . . Life the acid
wash that brought out the picture on what may
so truly be called a "negative" without it. . .
Experience!

"Is Happiness an answer or a seeking?" the
poet asks.

Everyone is, I think, consciously or uncon-
sciously, seeking for the Truth. Each one per-
ceives it from his own restricted angle; according
to his experience, his mental near or far-sighted-
ness; in part only as everything is seen and never
as a whole; just as I saw the shadows of the men
beside the campfire as mere silhouettes, the per-
ception of Truth limited to the individual capacity
for understanding. We comprehend it as little as

the flat fish with both eyes on one side of its head
can know the bottom of the ocean on which it rests.
And this, I think, is the answer to the multiplicity
of creeds.

When one has climbed so high one is close to
the great Amen, one realizes that each new experience is a door opened on to some treasure if he
has vision to see it; that life is the soul's chance to
grow. A night under the stars so high alters one.
Could one feel the universe seeming to pause in so
profound a peace and not stop with it and think?

The men were piling more fuel on the fire.
Their movement broke the spell and I became conscious of the cold night air.

I sought my cot. I crawled in with my clothes
on between sewed-up blankets and lay there gazing up at the stars. . . God's largesse cast across
the heavens. So still! So still! . . .

The ponies nosed about among the rocks, sometimes so close that I could touch them; the click
of their hoofs among the stones was the only audi-
ble sound in that immensity as the fire died down
to a mere glowing patch among the rocks.

But suddenly I could not breathe. I sat up with
some effort taking long straining breaths to drive
air further down into my lungs. With nothing to
lean against and on a cot that sagged down in the
middle I was too uncomfortable sitting up, and

the blankets pinned me down. Struggling for breath made my heart race madly . . . No air! No air! . . .

I snatched an ammonia tube from the pocket of my coat and broke it into my handkerchief. I felt better for awhile, then faint again and dizzy and gasping for breath. Would dawn never come!

At last! The sky was lighting up; the camp fire was stirred anew; "chota hazri" was being prepared for the sahibs before an early start. I crawled out of my cot, my head dizzy; "chota hazri" helped not at all. My poor little mare stood by, the foal at "chota hazri" also; she was less fit even than I for the steep climb; she stumbled up the embankment on to the road and I mounted . . . and turned back towards Leh.

"Another time . . . on a stronger pony, and straight through," I said to Sandy. So near the attainment of my goal; like so much that is undertaken in life:

> "But when your hope seems realized, to fall;
> To reach the path's rough end, and find a wall;
> To strive, to strain, with bitter years the cost
> And almost win . . . then find that you have lost."

CHAPTER XVII

ALONE IN LEH

SANDY and Margot spent the next day fishing. I went with Mrs. Berry to the palace of Senegge Namgyal which dominates the landscape around Leh. It is the first thing seen as one approaches, the last when one turns in the saddle for another look as one wends his way back to India. A sixteenth century building . . . and nine stories high . . . possibly the first skyscraper. It is a broad building, wider at the base and with broad windows and many balconies. It is reached by winding up the mountain, sometimes through dark lanes under houses, after leaving the bazaar. The palace is dark inside; stairways of stone lead on to roofs at several levels; one is liable to strike one's head mounting stairs and passing through doorways if one is not careful. A few rooms are handpainted, but badly done, and it is deserted now, for the King is a recluse in the monastery at Hemis and the Queen lives in Stock across the Indus River. Only the chapel of the palace is kept garnished, and here is the usual large statue of Buddha with silver

196

chorten, bowls of flowers, butter lamps, etc.   And there are books tucked into compartments along the walls, books that are long strips of paper stamped from wooden blocks or handlettered, the leaves held between strips of wood.

Around the central statue of Buddha was a row of tiny figures in niches, most of them draped in very old brocade which hid all but the little faces. There was one in particular that fascinated me, a Buddha with a tiny turquoise for the caste sign on his forehead.   The smiling lama in attendance permitted me to take it in my hand and unwrap the brocade and I found it to be a rarely beautiful thing, the border of its bronze robe etched elaborately, the modelling unusual.

It was very hot.   I must have touched my face which had on it many sand-fly bites, for the next morning my whole face was covered with running sores that burned and itched unbearably.

I called to Margot:

"Do send for Colonel Berry.   I've got the plague or something."   Colonel Berry came and reported that it would be impossible for me to travel to Kashmir until it was cured . . . sand and flies and heat would make the infection worse.

We had planned to go down that week.   I told them that they would have to go on without me; that I would follow later with Gulam.

This the Joint Commissioner forbade. But when it was learned that Bishop Peter of the Moravian Mission was going to Kashmir to meet his wife and bring her back to Leh Captain Falconer gave his permission for me to go down then also.

Sandy and Margot left at dawn next day, both of them stopping in my room to say good-bye.

"You'll find me in Calcutta . . . you have the address," said Margot.

"I'm always roaming," I remarked. "My interests are merely pastimes. We'll surely meet again."

"I'm anchored in Delhi. Do stop off there as you go through. It would be topping to see you. I'll do you well." So said Sandy.

After Margot and Sandy left Mrs. Falconer asked me to stay at the Residency until they went back to Srinagar, but I was quite comfortable at the bungalow and had no mind to tax their endurance too far by showing my face then.

Gulam and I settled down to housekeeping. He cooked my meals, saw that hot baths were provided and my room swept daily. He filled every wish of mine as soon as he understood it. Gulam. . . slave! The dak bungalow was empty but for myself. I was comfortable with an iron bed, good lounging chairs, an open fire, and books. . . .

THE ARCHITECTURE IN LEH WAS INTERESTING.

There was much talk about the Shyok Dam bursting at the time that I was in Leh. This is a transverse glacier which in its descent had blocked the Shyok River from bank to bank about twenty miles from its source up in the Karakorum Range north of Leh, and the probability of its bursting threatened the Indus River far down in India where the destruction of the bridge of Attock would have been a serious thing. The Punjab Government had sent an expert engineer, Mr. J. P. Gunn, to make a survey and to report conditions. With Mr. Ludlow, who was familiar with that territory, Mr. Gunn set out in May from Srinagar, crossed the Khardong Pass with coolie transport the end of June and found a lake of considerable size, which they estimated to be a thousand yards wide and about five hundred feet high, formed above the dam.

Before I left Leh Mr. Gunn returned with his caravan of yaks over the Khardong Pass and they caused great excitement in the compound where they unloaded. Yaks are enormous beasts with long shaggy hair and long horns. I had tried to get some of them to take my outfit up this same pass and failed.

Many of the wonderful photographs Mr. Gunn had taken he developed in his room in the dak bungalow and I had the pleasure of seeing them and hearing him talk about the lake of turquoise blue studded with glistening ice floes. The dam had finally broken but without the disastrous results that had been feared. . . .

Before Colonel and Mrs. Berry left I saw much of them. I dined with them and roamed about town with her. . . watched her painting bits of landscape. Sometimes I visited the Colonel in his hospital where he worked with his heart as well as his knowledge. A hospital in India is an extraordinary place. It was the same in Leh. Patients brought their families with them . . . as many members of it as possible. They set up housekeeping in the compound. . . cooked their own meals and lived as they might do at home.

And when Colonel and Mrs. Berry left I saw the heart of Leh. It happened like this:

The Joint Commissioner and Mrs. Falconer had already gone back to Kashmir and the time for Colonel Berry's departure had at last arrived. It was known that he would not return. Three summers of arduous labour in that high altitude was too wearing to be risked again. And because both he and Mrs. Berry had won the hearts of everyone the entire population turned out to bid them farewell. They encircled the little bungalow where the Berrys had lived for three months and the silence was tense until the door opened and Colonel and Mrs. Berry came out.

Then a girl came forward and prostrated herself in the dust at his feet and touched them reverently, tears streaming down her cheeks. He had saved her life a few weeks before when she nearly died from enteric.

The Colonel raised her up and she turned to Mrs. Berry pressing a turquoise ring into her hand. It was a simple thing, but her most prized possession. She could not pay in money, but she was grateful.

Other patients came and bent to the ground, one offering a tiny silver spoon, another a wee bowl . . . all they had. As the Colonel passed the hospital gate an old woman hobbled forward. She could hardly stand, for the leg that the Colonel had saved when blood poisoning set in after it had been mangled by an angry dog was still badly swollen. It was painful trying to kneel, but she too must take the dust from his feet. He patted her shoulder, and turning to me asked if I would see her daily and report her condition when I saw him as I expected to do ten days later on my way across the mountains. This translated to her brought tears of gratitude for his thoughtfulness.

On every side then people were weeping. Mrs.

Berry was struggling to hold back her tears, the Colonel looked as if he wanted to get away quickly before he too broke down. We marched through the main bazaar of Leh and out into the desert, the population following. It was very hot there although five o'clock in the afternoon and with fresh snow on the mountains about; it was hard going along rock-strewn paths, but the sorrowing multitude kept on.

I was reminded of that when I saw the Exodus scene in "Green Pastures" after my return home.

I stopped some distance out in the desert, said farewell to the Berrys and turned back to a silent city. The people I met had vacant bewildered faces; they were losing the greatest comfort that had ever come to them . . . skilled medical and surgical aid. They are grateful people, the Ladakhis.

CHAPTER XVIII

AND MORE OF LEH

NOTHING is something if you are doing it; which is not such a paradox as it sounds. I was fairly well occupied loafing the days away in a land where Time is a meaningless word about as important as the muted question of whether a hornet or a hippopotamus killed the first Egyptian King— Kheb meaning both hornet and hippo. What difference did hours make? The caravans could not get in this year? . . . Well maybe they would arrive next summer! Why did the sahibs always hurry so? They never stayed in any place for more than a few days at a time and it was good enough to lounge in the front of one's shop smoking a hookah . . . life andante.

I fell into the comfortable habit of not caring what time it was either. As the Japanese would say: "When my honourable insides became empty" I knew that it was time to eat, and whether I might be in my room or out under a tree in the compound, I would lift up my voice as they do in

India and call: "Quai Hai." This always brought
Gulam rushing, eager to fulfil my slightest wish:
"What did 'The Presence' desire?" And to the
order great or small always the answer: "Kassel!"
"You have spoken!"

I spent a night once in a paper doll's house in
Japan. They hurried just so to serve me when I
clapped my hands. They bowed to the earth before me, and I was said to "augustly condescend."
Now I was "The Presence." I thought of my
friends at home: A button pressed; an obsequious
waiter with expressionless face appearing. Not
for all the world would I have exchanged with
them.

Gulam did my cooking and meals arrived at
altogether uncertain hours and in uncertain quantities. I had what fresh vegetables could be purchased in the bazaar or from the bishop's garden,
but they were scarce and I had mostly to depend
on the few canned goods I had reserved from my
stores brought from Srinagar. My meals were
prepared over a fire on the floor of the cookhouse
across the compound. I had just two utensils, a
frying pan and a stew pan. I do not know how
Gulam managed to make scones, but they arrived
with each meal, probably baked in a cracker box.
Apricots were the only fresh fruit obtainable but
I found two jars of jam in the bazaar and the

bishop let me have some that he had made himself, so I got on famously.

Gulam even managed to procure a few logs of wood and made a fire in the grate in my room to take the early morning chill off. I slept comfortably in fur-lined sleeping socks that came above my knees and the long wool robe that had done service all along the route.

Sometimes I felt the altitude so badly that I could not rest lying down and sat in a chair most of the night breaking ammonia tubes into my handkerchief. These saved me from actual sickness and when they gave out, there being no drug store in Leh, I had recourse to aspirin and found that it worked just as well. The least exertion tired me. I found that I had to walk and talk very slowly and that if I stooped even to fasten my boots my heart palpitated violently. And I could not bear any restriction over my chest. But I was never actually ill. It was only that the altitude of 11,500 feet is trying during a six weeks' stay. One seems to feel it more the longer one remains; but it never prevented me from going about and even climbing the hills about Leh. I was actually growing stronger every day. . . .

I slept late mornings, then wandered about town or out into the desert, loving the quiet and the quaintness and friendliness of the place. Leh was so "homespun." I felt welcome and at home there. Every person I passed smiled and greeted me with "Zhu-le"; sometimes with tongue stuck out, but rarely, as this is not so much a custom in Ladakh as in Tibet proper. No one annoyed me, even by curiosity; there were no beggars in Leh; not even children followed me although they looked curiously enough at my camera when I took pictures. "Live and let live" seemed to be the motto of Ladakh.

It is a happy-go-lucky place where it would be impossible to tell the rich from the poor, for all wear the same garments of the same cut and weave, either homespun in narrow unbleached strips, or coloured maroon; sometimes of sateen in maroon or dark blue, and most of them look as if they had been worn for years. I had Gulam get a dark blue suit and it was lovely, the six-yard sash of red fringed at the end and wrapped many times around his slim waist. The entire garment was lined with cardinal red cloth which showed at the cuffs and at the collar which was bound with narrow gold braid. He wore baggy white trousers with it, and chaplies when outdoors. Indoors, as a respectful servant should, he went barefoot. And because he was a Mohamedan he wore the red fez that many wear instead of the native pagri or turban. . . .

Leh flaunted its welcome to you everywhere. Over the door of the leading curio shop were large letters W. C. which the owner thought was an abbreviation of this greeting. He was proud of his knowledge of English though that was as far as the attempt went and one shopped with gestures, which was rather fun.

Passing down the lanes I met the village belle, her cheeks covered with tiny yellow seeds that seemed to stick out of each pore . . . the Leh version of powder and rouge. I smiled when a merry youth greeted me, a flower behind his ear . . . the Ladakh buttonhole bouquet. I wanted to play with the happy and much loved babies that flop about in baskets on their mothers' backs or are carried on the backs of other children.

Leh shows something novel at every turn. One looks up and sees a goat hanging out of an upper story window or over the ledge of a roof, which is the garden of the house.

There seems to be little poverty in Leh, or rather the inhabitants have so few needs that they are easily supplied by the two crops a year yielded by fields well irrigated from streams flowing off the high snows. All of this country from the Pole down was eons ago covered with an ice cap, scientists relate. And some day the ice which has been steadily melting century by century will have vanished altogether and with it the rivers and streams and all will be desert like the Gobi instead of the happy hamlets that subsist easily now with scarcely any rainfall the year round.

There is little snow in Leh itself though the surrounding mountains may be covered with it and every access to it cut off by deep white blankets that hold from mid-October until May. Yet it is bitter cold during the winter months and consequently little washing is done. Fuel is scarce, fires expensive; it is warmer also to have the pores closed with an accumulation of dirt that makes one think the Ladakhi a dark-skinned race. . . .

In Leh there is no begging; there is no squalor, even the poorer quarters are clean; there is apparently no night life, and wandering through the bazaar at ten o'clock at night I found all houses in complete darkness . . . Leh slept. And more one might learn from Ladakh also . . . how to collect debts. And here it is done with a refinement of cruelty that is unconscious humour. After a creditor has exhausted other methods of collecting he simply takes up his abode with his debtor and never leaves him alone, he literally bores him to death; and if he be of higher caste he sends an agent to do so.

Wherever the debtor walks there also hovers his creditor, ready to explain to any listener why he, the debtor, should purchase nothing in the shops he visits; why he should not be relied on; why he is being shadowed. Let the debtor seek the peace of his home and the creditor enters with him, squats by the door watching him in silence that is occasionally broken with gentle reminders of the debt he owes. When sleep brings oblivion it lasts only until his eyes open again to find the creditor still beside him, and the distracted debtor at last turns the key in his strong box and wins his freedom.

The whole countryside is so utterly at peace that it is difficult to realize that there ever was a time when one needed a disguise to gain entrance to it as one Dr. Henderson had to do a hundred years ago. And now it is said of them by those who have lived years among them that they never steal, never lie, never murder and that infanticide is undreamed of and children so desired that should a woman wish to be rid of her babe there would be a hundred applicants for it in a land where polyandry restricts birth.

Women enjoy complete independence and I have read that Ladakh is the unique instance of a whole race adopting polyandry and adhering to it for hundreds of years. A girl marries the first two or three sons of a family, the eldest being credited with the parentage of any offspring. And

strangely enough there is no jealousy. When there
are no sons the daughter inherits and usually
marries a younger son who is called her "Magpa."
His would seem to be an unenviable position as
she may discard him at will and take thereafter
as many magpas as her fancy dictates.

I was the only remaining white person in Leh
except the Moravian Bishop who had lived there
for about thirty years.

The compound of the dak bungalow was open;
it was entered at all hours by all sorts of people;
I never locked my doors and they could have been
easily picked if I had. Everyone knew of course
that a white woman lived there alone without protection; with a servant to whom she could not even
talk. They knew it was one of those Americans
reputed to be fabulously rich, and there being no
bank in Leh that I must have money with me in
what to them would be an enormous sum for the
needs of such a journey and prolonged stay. Yet
I was never molested in any way. Not even
Gulam, who had constant access to my room, dis-
turbed one of my possessions. When I asked the
bishop about the safety of leaving money in my
yakdans he replied: "Leave it out on the porch
if you like. These people never steal."

I went freely everywhere knowing that I also
was absolutely safe. I wandered about the bazaar,

CHORTENS—THEIR TALL RED
SPIRES OUTLINED AGAINST
THE WHITE HOUSES.

DAWASHA SEATED ON HIS PORCH
MUMBLING PRAYERS.

THE MUCH DESIRED CHILDREN OF LEH.

SNOW PEAKS AT SASPUL THAT MELTED INTO THE DUSK LIKE
THINGS THAT SONGS ARE MADE OF.

APPARENTLY LOST—IN THE HIMALAYAS.

IT WAS BITTER COLD UNDER THE GLACIER OF MATCHOI.

up dark lanes, and after the heat of the day, far
out into the desert. There it was so lovely with
wide sweeps of sand running down from high
ridges outlined against snow ranges on every side,
Leh lying like a bunch of marabout among the
willow groves at their base. There were snow-
storms on the mountains during those peaceful
weeks, and the air was bracing after the sun went
down. My flashlight showed the way across stepping stones and narrow bridges when it grew dark,
and I could jump the rivulets that trickled from
field to field. I loved it best at dusk, the solemnity
of religious music coming from some nearby
gompa where the lamas chanted prayers and the
great shawms wove their spell around me.

Through the day songs reached me from fields
where men and women were harvesting. It was
then September. Huge stacks of grain were tied
about with native homespun ropes. Men bent
their backs to them, drew the ends of rope across
their shoulders and, rocking back and forth until
the burden was lifted, carried it off. And the song
they sang, and the song that all the men and
women at work in the fields sang, a constantly
repeated bar, was this:

"The sun is bright, the burden is light." Coué in Ladakh.

Architecture in Leh is quaint. Houses are broad at the base, the eaves often decorated. The tops of the windows project, and the windows are sometimes closed with lattice-work. Roofs are stacked with lucerne and everywhere there are prayer flags fluttering from slender poles. One sees splashes of red on the corner of houses . . . that is to ward off the Evil Spirit. Or there will be a ram's head hung over the doorway for protection against the spirits of the air. Sometimes a row of three small chortens are set high in a shrine and profusely decorated and coloured red, white and blue. The end of lanes show vistas of chortens, their tall red spires distinct against the white houses, and chortens track far out into the desert beside mané walls heaped with prayer stones engraved with the mantra: "Om mané padme hum."

Living in that isolation with them I could understand the fear of the supernatural that gripped them; their desire to placate the spirits of evil whose manifestations of power seemed to be in evidence on all sides . . . in the flooded streams that season after season tore bridges away; in avalanches that hurled themselves from on high without warning; in landslides that obliterated paths and carried man and beast to destruction.

What was left for helpless creatures to do but win protection through the intercession of the lamas whose business it is to placate Evil Spirits and who rule by power of numbers, unity of effort, and spiritual control? Lamas are paid to cut the sacred mantra into stones, to recite from the holy writ, to twirl prayer wheels. Church-going as we understand it does not exist—that is the lama's business.

Just below the dak bungalow is the house of a prominent merchant, Dawasha, to whom is yearly entrusted the carrying of tribute to the Dalai Lama at Lhasa. Through the day and through the night at regular intervals a bell tolls from his house; a lama chants from the sacred scriptures; Dawasha pays to gain merit. From his housetop floats a prayer flag; the main room in his house is a chapel, open like a pavilion onto the porch. In it is an altar of red and gold whereon are sacred vessels and relics in an exquisite reliquary studded with turquoise. The bowls are of silver, the holy water pitcher is draped with brocade, gold-fringed, and an empty C. & C. Ginger Ale bottle I found prominent among these sacred objects, important no doubt because of the label. The walls are hung with priceless handpainted banners, exquisite in colour and in workmanship, and along two sides of the wall are low cushions of Chinese rugs and a row of low folding tables of beautiful design.

Dawasha's house is gaily painted like a Chinese pagoda outside and in, and there he received me when the bishop took me to call on him; and there he posed for his picture sitting behind a low table mumbling prayers, beside him the vessels for religious service, a teapot with embossed rim and spout set deep in turquoise. He was a kindly host and showed me the kitchen of his home where rows of highly polished brass and copper pitchers and bowls stood on shelves. A low stove was built in clay from the ground to about two feet in height. It was a wide affair, with fire in a grate on the floor into which the large nozzle of a bellows was inserted, pushed well under the glowing fuel. The bellows were made of a goat-skin sack operated by a fire-blower whose sooty face was lifted to me in a cheerful smile. The stove was inset with blue and red stones at the side. About the room stood huge churns for butter-tea which is thick like soup.

Sometimes the bishop invited me to a meal in his garden, and there his fire was out-of-doors; bellows kept the flame glowing; a pot stewed with good German food. And his "chupatties" eaten with the stew were delicious, and his kindliness appreciated in that far mountain region . . . in the highest capital city in the world.

CHAPTER XIX

WHAT I LEARNED FROM BOOKS

In Leh is the Legend of Christ who is called "Issa," and it is said that the monastery at Hemis holds precious documents fifteen hundred years old which tell of the days that He passed in Leh where He was joyously received and where He preached. There is also the tradition of the biblical flood. And they have a National Epic of which only a few manuscripts exist and no printed copies. Almost every village recites its own version of the story, for there are yet village bards in the land and they tell of the King of Heaven who was asked to send one of his sons to be King of Earth, and of the mission of his youngest son to Earth.

Tibetans seem to have originated the Darwin theory for they claim as their first parent a monkey which crossed the Himalayas and there married a She-Devil of the mountains.

These things and much else I learned from books as I loafed the days away under the shade of willows. But the most interesting thing I read

about was the similarity between the vestments
and ceremonials of Buddhism and those of the
Catholic Church. This has often been noted by
other writers. The Christian Church took over the
dates of pagan festivals for its feast days, and its
vestments were the garments familiar to that age.
What link there is between the ceremonials and
the date of adoption I have not seen stated. It
seemed strange to find in that out of the way
corner of the earth not only the rituals of Buddhism as known in India but much besides that was
peculiar to the Catholic Church without there being
a corresponding similarity of belief. The time
since my trip has been too short for much research
but I give here a few striking examples of the
similarity mentioned:

There is the constant effort to "gain merit" by
means similar to those used by Catholics to gain
indulgences; there is the Rosary of 108 beads
divided into sets of tens with a large bead dividing
them and three beads at the end symbolizing the
Buddhist Trinity: Buddha, The Word, and The
Church. In "This Believing World" by Lewis
Brown I read on my return to America: "Christians did not learn of the Rosary until they observed
its use during the Crusades among the Moslems;
but the Moslems themselves had only a little earlier

first taken to it as a sacred symbol in imitation of the followers of the God Shiva." The Catholic version given in the "Lives of the Saints" is that Saint Dominic received it from the Blessed Virgin in 1208 as he knelt at prayer in the chapel of Notre Dame de la Prouille.

In Buddhism are found also the perpetual lamp before the altar, incense and vessels identical with those used in Catholic Churches; holy water and the holy water font, fasts, asceticism, grace before food, chanted prayers, confession, communion, extreme unction, the chalice and paten, consecrated bread and wine, mitres, copes, images, holy pictures, scapulars, amulets that take the place of medals, votive offerings, relics, censers, choirs, the bell during religious service, tonsured monks, celibacy of the clergy, nuns, abbots, cardinals, a pope, hermits, saints, good and evil spirits, litanies, the sign of the cross, pastoral crooks, indulgences, which they call "gaining merit," by acts of devotion or the repetition of the prayer "Om mané padme hum."

I have before me some Catholic leaflets from: "A Little Treasury of Indulgenced Prayers": "While looking reverently at the Sacred Host, the words recited: 'My Lord and My God!' Seven years and seven quarantines and a plenary indulgence once a week for those that have recited this prayer every day."

"For saying: 'Jesus in the Blessed Sacrament have mercy on us' 100 days Indulgence."

"For making some exterior sign of respect when passing before a church or an oratory in which the Most Blessed Sacrament is reserved, an Indulgence of 100 days."

Other Indulgences are promised for genuflecting before the tabernacle on one knee and on both knees, and a plenary indulgence at the hour of death for another simple act of homage done while in perfect health.

To quote Lewis Brown again: "Christianity began to have its effect first through the efforts of the early Nestorian preachers and much later through the activities of Protestant missionaries. Buddhism in Tibet very early took on a distinct Christian colouring accepting into its ritual such Christian symbols as the cross, the mitre, the dalmatica, censer, chaplet, and holy water font, etc."

The use of holy water in the Christian church goes back to the sixth century, but the pope's tiara, which was part of Byzantine court dress, was first used by the popes in the eighth century, and it was that century which saw Padma Sambhava bringing Buddhism into Tibet from India, finding in Tibet not any particular kind of religion but a fairly savage people. It was he who instituted Lamaism which is a form of Buddhism.

Kublai Khan, the Chinese Emperor who was friend to Marco Polo, called a great assembly of the most powerful Lamaist Hierarchs to his court together with representatives of Christian and other faiths, to determine which religion was best suited to weld together the more uncivilized portions of his great empire. He ultimately chose Lamaism as the best for that purpose and it was he who set up the head of the Lamaist Church with temporary powers as tributary ruler of Tibet. That was towards the end of the thirteenth century. Under the fifth Grand Lama, and at his request, a Mongolian prince conquered Tibet and made him a present of it and in the middle of the seventeenth century he was confirmed in his sovereignty by the Chinese Emperor and given the Mongol title of Dalai or "vast" (as the ocean).

Friar Oderic in the early fourteenth century is said to be the first European to visit Lhasa and an Austrian Jesuit and a Belgian Count went there centuries later. In the eighteenth century the Capuchin Fathers and the Jesuits settled there and the mission lasted for half a century.

Much of this information was gleaned from that most absorbingly fascinating book "Lamaism in Tibet" by Waddell. It would be interesting reading if there could be assembled into one record proofs of the assumption of rituals by all the various religions, and this might include Iconography as well.

CHAPTER XX

BACK ALONE ACROSS THE HIMALAYAS

THE Moravian Bishop of Leh had planned to leave there for Srinagar on September fourteenth. Before he left, the British Joint Commissioner had exacted a written guarantee that I would journey down at the same time. This relieved him of all responsibility for me.

But I knew that I should virtually make the trip across the mountains alone. Though the bishop might be on the road at the same time we should not be together since he was an experienced traveller and knew the passes, and could ride fast on his big Mongolian horse. It would be impossible for me to keep up with him on the horse he was taking in for his wife to ride home on. This he kindly offered me with the stipulation that I must keep close at his heels. It was not to be expected that he would adapt himself to my snail's pace.

As it would take me longer than it would take him to cover the distances between stages I should need to start long before he got up each day, and for that reason I made up my own "bandobast" separate from his. I needed to keep my little outfit with me, or on ahead of me, as my ponies carried all of my equipment, while the bishop had sufficient conveniences along with him in his saddle bags and could let his ponies wander into camp at will.

This proved to be a wise move, for when he stopped at Matayan, I had to make the further stage of Matchoi. And later I left him altogether and went on two or three days ahead of him while he delayed for necessary telegraphic information at Sonamarg.

Still there was a measure of protection in travelling down the same day as the bishop. Had I not arrived at the end of any day he could have sent a man back along the road to ascertain the cause of my delay. But if he were miles away from me, he could not help to prevent any of the accidents I feared, the misstep or stumbling of my pony on a rock ledge or the sudden fright of my steed. Nothing could save me then from being hurled over the precipice. Also I dreaded the possible washing away of the trails and the inevitable fordings . . . the dilemma of what best to do when there would be no one to take council with. Gulam could not understand English. The floods too, I feared. They had been severe. That

THE FIRELIGHT REFLECTED ON
GULAM'S EAGER FACE.

MY SMALL CARAVAN CROSSING THE SNOW BEDS OF THE ZOJI-LÀ.

RETURNING ALONE WITH MY CARAVAN OVER THE ZOJI-LÀ.

RETURNING ALONE WITH MY LITTLE CARAVAN—A FOOTHOLD
ON ROCK LEDGES.

GULAM PITCHES MY TENT AT GUND.

THE ROAD WAS SOMETIMES ALL ROCKS.

presaged landslips and necessitated fordings. How much of the trail was left no one knew for no one had been over the trail for many days when I journeyed down. I dreaded the dark gorge where the trail ran beside the river. I dreaded most going down over the snow beds and rock ledges of the Zoji-Là alone.

But fear is a great emotion. It would be the greater experience for a woman to journey for two hundred and fifty miles across the Himalayas alone. If I got through safely, I should be more gratified for having made it by myself.

I arranged for four pony men to accompany my five pack ponies in order that loading in the early morning hours might be quicker. The ponies needed assistance up and down steep grades as well as in the event of meeting caravans from the opposite direction. To pass another pony on the narrow rock cuttings is difficult.

Instead of counting on the Res Transport, which would have meant a change of ponies each day, I arranged to take part of the same large caravan that furnished eleven pack ponies to the bishop, who was transporting three hundred Tibetan books to Srinagar, to ship them from there to a university in Germany. This caravan had come into Leh from Kashmir with bales of goods and was glad to have a return load.

They charged only twelve rupees per pony for the entire two hundred and fifty miles instead of the regulation fifteen which the changes of Res Transport averaged. This was about $4.45 instead of $5.55. I had sent back to Dras for the little Balti pony I had ridden from there to Kargil on the way out and arranged with his owner to pay forty rupees a month for him or about $11.00 and this included his pony man and food for them both. It was a better arrangement than trusting to the poor specimens that would be brought in each day when I could not even state my requirements to the tehsildars.

When I had let my bandobast go back to Srinagar three weeks earlier I had retained for myself one of the eight by eight tents and a servant's pal or small tent for my men; also a folding canvas cot and chair, a few kitchen things and necessary stores. Kadera and Happy went back with my bandobast and my bearer Gulam was to be guide, bearer and manager of my outfit. This consisted of eight ponies in all, three of these being riding horses for myself and servants. There were seven men: the four pony boys for the pack ponies, my own pony boy, Gulam and a Ladakhi who wanted to go to Kashmir and undertook to be sweeper for me at the rate of thirty rupees, double what is paid for this service everywhere in India and Kashmir.

Before Colonel Berry left Leh he had admonished Gulam to take good care of me and had transmitted to him the instructions I gave about keeping the pack ponies along with me, etc. . . . Later when I needed to speak to Gulam I took him down to the bishop's quarters and he translated what I said into Ladakhi.

I was nevertheless a bit nervous at starting out alone from Leh with seven men unable as I was to speak to one of them, having to rely on sign language in any emergency that might arise. Gulam spoke a little Urdu and I thought it well to learn a few words of it myself before the journey and so I had the local schoolmaster come up for an hour each day to teach me the few words and sentences that I might need along the road.

I learned that a horse was "Goré"; drinking water "Pine-ki-pani"; how to say hot and cold, and how to tell my men that they must be ready to march at "saré ché bujji" or half past six, and to come to me and hold my horse while I dismounted when I called "Goré kô pakro."

I might have saved myself the effort, for on the trip I found it advisable to have Gulam ride on ahead to show the road which was sometimes washed away requiring wide detours and repeated fordings back and forth across the rivers to find whatever foothold offered on either side.

This left me with only the Balti pony man at hand. He was not familiar with Urdu and when I first called: "Goré kô pakro," he thought that he must do something in response and whipped up my pony over a nasty bit that I had intended to negotiate on foot. We then came to an understanding that he was to come when I used the one word "pakro." This I taught him by repeating the word and making signs. I had learned on the way out that one clucked to a horse to make him halt and beckoned people to one when one desired that they should go the opposite way.

I felt confident of Gulam's loyalty, for he had served me well during six weeks but I was not sure that he would remember the route among the mountains as he had crossed them only once before. I liked the pony men who engaged to go with the caravan, for they were a cheerful lot and the leader, an older man, seemed to take a real pride in meeting my wishes. When he came to ask me any favour he raised his clasped hands as in prayer. Somehow we made each other understand a little. I felt absolute trust in all of them. I was not sure of the sweeper who had a large knife in his belt and a beard that hid his features, but he was a

Ladakhi, and that meant much. My pony man I did not like. And so much could happen along the road while he would be the only one of the outfit constantly near me. . . .

I was dressed and watching the loading of my ponies before dawn on September fourteenth. In Kashmir packs are laid across strips of gunny which holds them firmly when they are strapped to the long padded Kashmiri pack saddle, whereas in Ladakh goods are merely laid across double ropes made of yak's hair and strapped to the same wooden saddles that are used for riding . . . a much more cumbersome and less secure method. But things move slowly in that corner of the world and the same costumes and equipment and means of transportation that Marco Polo found are in use to-day.

Within the first hour of my trek my caravan was halted three times by the shifting of an unwieldy pack and this gave the bishop, who had not even started to load his ponies when I stopped to wish him good morning as I passed his house, time to catch up with me before I had gone five miles. I had started out wearing ill-fitting chaplies that had lost what shape they originally had in the constant wettings of the trip out, and one makes better headway on foot through the rock-strewn desert. I was trudging along enjoying the streaks of light on the mountains, as the sun climbed high over the slopes of grey-brown that shaded into red, with towering snow peaks and glaciers showing beyond. I was not so careful as I should have been in stepping among the stones and stubbed my toe and fell flat, striking my chin against a rock which scraped and bruised it badly.

The medicine chest was well on ahead on one of the pack ponies. I did not dare even to wipe my chin for fear of infection, and I was delighted when the bishop rode up on his beautiful Mongolian horse and offered me the use of another one that he was taking in for his wife to ride back on. I thus covered much of the desert stretch at a faster gait than my little Balti pony could have managed. But being the very worst rider on record I soon had to transfer back to my own little pony whose short legs made slower progress, as the gait the bishop's horse took as soon as the desert tract was free of stones was one that I could not keep up for long.

And so I ambled on, alone but for Gulam and my pony man. Now and then a red-robed lama passed on horseback, his high yellow cap pointed up at the ears, a bit of colour in the sandy waste. . . .

I was tired and badly burned when I arrived at

Niemu at two in the afternoon and was glad to
have the cup of tea that the bishop offered, he
having got in long ahead of me. A strong wind
part of the way had driven particles of sand into
the sore on my chin and I was glad of the supply
of peroxide in my medicine chest. In Leh the
thermometer had registered 50° in the afternoon;
at Niemu it was 70°, and so long had the dak
bungalow been closed that when I opened a window in my room a cloud of tiny moths flew out of
the red flannel curtains literally covering me and
my effects. I can almost claim now that I am
moth-eaten.

My six weeks of idleness in Leh did not make
riding easier now and I was glad that I had my
bedding roll at hand to turn in at once and rest
before the evening meal. Then there was interesting conversation with Bishop Peter while our
separately cooked meals were served and a long
night of sleep in glorious quiet which set me quite
on my feet again for the start next day at dawn.

I had gone some distance on the road to Saspul
next day when the bishop rode up and I had
another stretch on his large horse. But he was
the stable mate of the beautiful Mongolian and
insisted on following close at the latter's heels;
when we descended sharp zigzags the bishop's

horse would quicken his pace as he reached the
level, and my mount would do likewise on the
twisting, downward path which was a bit more
than my nerves would stand. I preferred the
sober methods of my own little pony who after
all got me to Saspul in time for a good long rest
in the afternoon.

While my bedding roll was being unfolded by
Gulam I enjoyed some of the bishop's chupatties
and coaxed him to eat some of Gulam's well-cooked
food when my repast was ready. The bishop and
I seldom ate at the same time. He carried
everything necessary for his meals along with him
in saddle bags on his own and his bearer's horse
while I had everything carried on my pack ponies.

At Saspul it was lovely at dusk. Sitting on the
upper verandah one looked over a range of snow
peaks that melted into the darkness like things
that songs are made of; below, in the compound,
our saddle horses were tethered. I fed the Mongolian some of the sugar with which I enticed good
behaviour from my Balti. He took it as daintily
as a person might have done, slowly and carefully,
while my pony grabbed for it and showed every
sign of annoyance that there was not more. I
have never seen so magnificent an animal as the
bishop's Mongolian; large, powerful, slant-eyed;
with all the tricks of a bucking bronco during life's

ordinary routine, he seemed to know that the road meant business and was as docile as a lamb.   The bishop said that I might ride him with perfect confidence . . . I preferred not to. . . .

The next day was uneventful.   Then the Bishop got off ahead of me from Nurla, the following stage, as he was to spend the day in Khalatsi with Dr. and Mrs. Kuenick of the Moravian Mission there with whom he had business to transact. I delayed my start hoping to arrive in Khalatsi after the morning meal was over, but I found them all at table when I rode in. Colonel and Mrs. Berry were there also, he having stopped to tend the sick in the neighbourhood. I enjoyed an hour with them, wishing that it might be longer for the Kuenicks have an atmosphere about them that belongs to those high places and their name is blessed throughout the countryside. But the long dark Lamayuru Gorge lay ahead and I had to traverse it alone not knowing what wash-outs there might be.

Caravans are rare at that season and there were no reports on the condition of the road; and between those giant cliffs, along a ledge cut in their face, with the Indus River below swollen from summer rains, one might easily be trapped by a break in the road or a landslide making progress impossible where no detour could be achieved. It was hardly practical to spend the night on the rock ledge, so I must push on before dark caught me there.

Mrs. Berry walked the long hot road down to the Indus and across the bridge with me, and there we parted and I hurried on with just my pony man and Gulam, my caravan having gone on ahead while I visited in Khalatsi. Gulam rode on testing the road to warn me of possible breaks that might surprise me at sharp bends. I wondered what would happen if one did occur as I had no words in my vocabulary to cope with such a situation. But "chance" is the password of the road, and all around me was such grandeur and majesty that it absorbed me to the exclusion of all anxiety.

The road wound through dark lonely hills that shut one in. Stupendous rocks overhung the path and shut out all but occasional glimpses of the sun. It was brooding, silent, mysterious, and so varied even in its sombreness. The churning river was now but a few feet below the road, then, as this mounted, a mere streak, its voice the only sound beside the click of the ponies' heels against the stones of the rock path. I had thought the gorge beautiful as I descended into it on the way out, but now when the road finally mounted to the light I felt as I did once when coming up out of the pit of a coal mine. Only it took longer to mount the two thousand feet out of the deepest gorge in the world at Lamayuru. I arrived on its brink when day was fading.

For a few miles next day I rode the bishop's extra horse across the Fotu Là when he caught up with me as usual after my earlier start. But I went back to my own pony long before the next stage was reached. I waited some time on the crest of the Fotu Là alone; hating to leave; each step dragging me nearer to a world that somehow I did not seem to fit into any more.

I came at twilight to Bod Kharbu to find the bishop smoking his pipe on the porch as if he had been at home there for a week. He had finished his evening meal, and I had my dinner of sardines and canned vegetables and scones and tea outdoors by such brilliant moonlight that no lantern was necessary.

At Bod Kharbu pariah dogs prowled about all night. It was cold enough to have frozen the germ of original sin in me. But fleas seem to be weather-proof and I discovered that Bod Kharbu was a lively spot.

Next day I had an exhilarating ride up the Na-mika Là on the big horse. A cold wind sang in my ears and frost bit my face though I was well muffled in wool. So much dust blew into my eyes that even at that early hour I put on my sun glasses with side-shields.

Everything looked different riding towards the east and it was easier going as the general trend was down grade. But I could not hold the pace and the bishop rode on ahead once more. The route was so familiar to him that it held no enchantment. His thought was to get to the next stage as soon as possible and be comfortable, whereas I hated to leave each new beauty on the road, and though I was tired, I was then so fit that the going was easier and I had never need to stop over even for a day.

At Moulbe Gulam came to me holding his "tummy" with both hands and imitating the gurgling sound it made. Jamaica ginger cured him while Eno's Fruit Salts restored the bloom of health to my other men and there was no delay in starting next morning.

It was very bleak at Moulbe. A snowstorm was sweeping across the mountains when the bishop and I started out, this time together. It was a beautiful sight at dawn. There was a bitter cold wind and I was thankful for my heavy sweater and flannel-lined woollen homespun suit; for the extra short skirt that wrapped around my riding breeches, and for fur gloves and two pairs of woollen stockings inside my fur-lined Gilgit boots.

It was much too cold to ride until the sun was well up and we trudged by our horses to keep circulation going, a cruel wind biting our faces. But with the sun high it was too hot and I had to change to summer outfit. The coolie carrying the large canvas bag which held my clothes was always close at hand.

The bishop was making fast time to Kargil, the next stage, where I did not expect to see him at all as he had to meet some missionaries there and expected to stay with them instead of at the dak bungalow. He rode on ahead after awhile and Gulam and I, instead of striking the high road above the river that I had come by on the way out, took to the bed of what was in September only a shallow stream.

But soon it widened and swept over the lower road and we were forced to leave the broken embankment and ride the river bed. We got well wet in crossing to the opposite side, only to have to repeat the manœuvre as the paths on both sides had been obliterated. When the water became too deep we set our horses at the bank and mounted to follow what was no longer a road but the general direction towards Kargil.

The day was far advanced; the country entirely unfamiliar-looking; and as we plodded on and on with no landmark that I had seen on the out journey I became convinced that Gulam had lost his way. I thought that he had somehow got on the other side of the mountain and that, my pack ponies having gone on ahead, night would find us with no food or shelter, and apparently lost . . . somewhere in the Himalayas.

I could not talk to Gulam. Why, oh why had I not thought to learn a sentence in Urdu covering such an emergency!

Then I recalled a word meaning good or well and with a question in my voice called to Gulam:

"Gulam . . . *teak?*"

He nodded his head.

But would he admit it if he really had lost his way? Perhaps he was pretending and just hoping to find the road.

There was no one in sight for him to ask advice of and it certainly looked entirely different to me from any road I had traversed on the way out. Not even the bagh at Paskyum where we had camped was in sight, yet surely we had been on the road long enough to have passed it.

Again I questioned:

"Gulam . . . *teak?*" "Kargil?" waving my hand towards the distance ahead.

Again he nodded.

I felt as the sailors with Columbus must have felt . . . not so sure as he was.

At least if we kept on going we must arrive somewhere I figured and there was nothing else to do anyway. How fortunate to have thought of the word *teak*. I used it on all occasions thereafter; with a nod and a smile to indicate that I was pleased; with a shake of the head and a frown and "nay teak" if dissatisfaction was to be registered. It worked beautifully and the old pony man beamed as I did when at last we had established a means of communication.

Finally I spied a familiar landmark and then a sharp up-grade to the wide Kargil plateau which I had not appreciated on the way out in the early morning. How beautiful it was! The vast high plain was encircled by snow clad peaks that rose to enormous heights. The river was far below. Sunset painted rainbow colours along the ridges long before we reached the dak bungalow. I had come twenty-three miles without stopping except for a brief time for lunch at noon, this a hard boiled egg, jam, biscuits and tea carried by my one coolie. It was dusk when we dropped down into the compound of the dak bungalow at Kargil—the half way station, and I bethought me of an expressive word so often heard down in India:

"Shabash!" Gulam understood that it meant "Bravo!"

How he managed to get water carried up that

steep hill from the river I do not know, for I had no regular bishti. But in no time at all I heard him pouring hot water into the tub in my bathroom and when I was refreshed there was a good hot meal ready for me; scones, canned vegetables and canned fruit and sausages.

I had the large dak bungalow all to myself and was surprised when some time later the bishop rode in, he having found no quarters available with the missionaries in Kargil.

My old pony man had sore eyes. I used to drop boric acid into them each day as he lay with his head on the step of the bungalow. It relieved him and he was very grateful. All of the men made inroads into my medicine chest which is a rarity along the road and I fancy endowed with some sort of magic in their opinion. . . .

Next day there was a river to ford where the bridge had been washed away in the summer floods. Then we had to go up the rock shelving where my pony had shied on the way out. It seemed to be a fated spot, for here the bishop's pack ponies caught up with my small outfit and none of us saw the caravan arriving from the opposite direction as they wound up the steep rock path. They were upon us before we could halt them, more and more ponies pushing up from behind, and there was confusion.

Such shouting and pulling of ponies into every

available crevice in the rocks to avoid their being pushed instead into the river!

Gulam and the bishop, who had come up with his outfit, ran ahead shouting warnings to stop the oncoming pack train and so prevent the ponies from shoving each other over the embankment.

I slipped off my pony as he was wedged in between rocks and crawled up onto a boulder from which I took motion pictures while my pony man struggled to clear the path for me.

The bishop and his caravan then outdistanced us and when I rode into Shimshi Kharbu, the next halting place, it was with an officer who had come in from Skardo across the suspension bridge beyond Kargil where he had been shooting.

The fields were being harvested as I rode on to Dras alone next day; plodding teams thrashed golden grain; bales were tossed high by men and women who chanted in unison as do the boatmen by the Jhelum River bank in Kashmir. It was cool all along the road that day and at Dras I found the dak bungalow all dressed up in a fresh coat of paint and there the bishop with his welcome cup of tea waiting for me.

My medicine basket was again in demand. People came in from the town to ask aid for all sorts of ailments. One of my pony men had cut his hand deeply, and from there on I had daily dressings to perform, knowing nothing better to use than peroxide and unguentine. But my handling of the sanitary gauze and cotton wool on the tips of my scissors, and winding the bandage in an impressive way, although not in approved style, was the source of great wonder and interest. It made an important occasion each evening and although the bandage was filthy within a short while luckily no infection set in and the wound healed rapidly.

After Dras I was no more with the bishop. He halted at Matayan, about seventy-seven miles or more from Srinagar, while I pushed on nine miles farther to the tiny dak bungalow at Matchoi. I did not wish to have that tiresome journey to add to the necessary descent over the dread Zoji-Là the next day, a journey which would have taken me thirteen hours to make had I stopped with the bishop at Matayan.

It was bitter cold at Matchoi under the glacier. Gulam was able to secure a few logs to make a fire in my room but it was impossible to heat water for a bath; a practical demonstration of the reason for lack of cleanliness in the natives of those parts.

My men suffered greatly from the cold; the sweeper coughed all night and complained of illness, for icy gales swept down from the Matchoi glacier which rose to 17,686 feet just above the dak bungalow. The officer who had come in onto

the road from Skardo marched in late in the afternoon and we exchanged news and magazines and
tinned goods.   He was going over the Zoji and
turning off at Baltol for barasing hunting. Barasing is a species of deer. I was going to head straight
for Sonamarg.

From Matchoi we started together at dawn with
a bitter cold wind blowing and the officer soon outdistanced me. I stopped by the roadside just beyond the watershed of the Zoji later to have a cup
of hot tea with him beside his crackling fire, then
left him and went on down the Four Devil Pass
alone. The bishop passed me with his caravan
when I was halfway across it. There were no flowers along the pass now, no edelweiss. But the
blanket of snow still held fast between stark cliffs
and my small pack train crossed it and wound its
way down along the rock ledges just ahead of me
and into the wooded country below where everything was green and trees once more covered the
mountain sides.

I found the bishop comfortably settled in the
dak bungalow at Sonamarg when I arrived there
after having covered fifteen miles since dawn over
the snow beds of the Zoji-Là and the dreaded pass
alone. There were two rooms in the rest house but
the bishop said that the remaining one had been
reserved for another man so I pitched my tent

some distance away beside the high bank of the
Sind River, and had tea with the bishop while my
men set up camp. He later came over to visit me
and to say good-bye as I should start early next
morning and should not see him again for several
days. He remained over to wait for telegraphic
messages from his wife, for at Sonamarg is a post
and telegraph office.

After I had turned in I had to call Gulam to
tighten my tent ropes for a sudden high wind came
up and nearly sent it over the embankment into the
river. The camp fire also had to be extinguished
as sparks were flying dangerously about the canvas. . . .

Long before dawn I heard my men moving and
the ponies being driven in from the hills and loaded.
The ground was covered thick with frost. A river
crossing had to be made and this along a single log
thrown across the stream, a log round and slippery
which I negotiated sideways while my pony was
driven across.

Then the path climbed a slippery bank along a
cow path that made a wide detour, as the whole of
the route traversed through Gagangair Gorge in
July had been washed out by the floods that had
wrought havoc in Kashmir. I travelled further in-
land missing the gorge and crossing fields into the

heart of pine forests where it was cool amidst the flitting shadows.

Gone were all the wild flowers. The river was strewn with wreckage. Floating logs dammed the streams. Stones, over which my pony had to pick his way carefully, covered the once fertile fields, swept down by spates from the mountains that now were covered with snow. We mounted high, looking down on the devastation of the countryside.

Occasionally a man passed carrying an inflated goatskin full of food or drink. Sometimes the way was blocked by what looked to be a hay stack until one noticed the brown legs beneath, which soon made way for us. The detour added two hours to the march which was hard going as much of it had to be made on foot and my feet had been badly blistered descending the steep grade of the Zoji-Là. I was glad when at last my tent was pitched beneath the walnut trees at Gund. . . .

I loved it there, better than ever on the return journey. The river rushed noisily below the steep bank. Gulam bent over my improvised stove concocting out of apparently nothing at all a delicious meal for me. The firelight reflected on his eager face accentuated his high cheek bones.

Gulam never once complained of heat or cold or fatigue; he was up long before dawn rousing the pony men; starting a fire that I might have hot tea and also warm water to bathe in. He pitched my tent, supervised loading and unloading; in every respect what would be called in those parts a "pukka bandobast-walla." I had got so used to him that it seemed hard to believe that the great adventure was nearing its end. I felt that it would be more natural to expect that life would go on in this way always.

My men sat around the camp fire passing the hookah, eating their meagre repast, chatting . . . I wondered what about. They were all at home in a bleak treeless country and about them here were pine covered mountains and spreading branches hung over them. In Kashmir nature is prodigal.

I had come back across the mountains much quicker than I had gone out and on the fourteenth day after leaving Leh was already in Kangan, the last stage for me before Srinagar.

I did not go into Ganderbal. I had telegraphed from Sonamarg for the motor lorry that met me at Weyil Bridge and carried me the remaining miles to town.

Here I paid off my pony men who took the dust from my feet in gratitude for the inadequate "baksheesh" which custom dictated, with a bit over because they had cared so faithfully for me.

At Kangan the cicadas hummed in the trees; the

chanting songs of natives at work filled the air. From there, on the 28th of September, I had to make another wide detour up a steep cliff where the sides of the path were protected by a railing. I looked down into the beautiful Vale of Kashmir. The journey was over. The passes would soon be closed with snow. My men would turn back to the daily repetition of a hard life while I would go on across more mountains and across oceans to a life of variety and ease and interest.

Yet, be one ever so much of a sybarite, loving all silken things, once the Himalayas have had one in their grip they will call and call . . . for those wild lonely passes hold one in "the bond that shall last 'till the crows turn white and the glaciers melt," as they would say in Ladakh. And there on the brink of civilization I hesitated:

"Shall I leave the hills, the high, far hills
   That shadow the morning plain?
Shall I leave the desert sand and sage
    that gleams in the winter rain?
Shall I leave the ragged bridle-trail
    to ride in the city street——
To snatch a song from the printed word
Or sit at a master's feet?

To barter the sting of the mountain winds
   for the choking fog and smoke?

To barter the song of the mountain stream
   for the babble of city folk?
To lose my grip on the God I know
   and fumble among the creeds?
Oh rocks and pines of the high, far hills,
Hear the lisp of the valley reeds!"

APPENDIX

The best time to make the trip to Leh is in June.

Kashmir is easily reached by through train from Bombay or Calcutta to the end of the line at Rawal Pindi. There a motor is easily procured at the station or hotel for the ride into Srinagar, Kashmir. The fare first class from Bombay to Rawal Pindi is Rs. 125, or about $46.25, and Rs. 9.6 or about $3.50 for bearers fare third class. From Calcutta it costs less. A motor into Kashmir costs between 80 and 125 rupees according to the season and the car.

Indian Bradshaws giving all trains throughout India with mileage and costs and a map are procurable at any bookstore. Travel in India is exceedingly comfortable. One's bearer handles all luggage. One should procure a bedding roll before starting.

Nedou's is the only hotel in Srinagar. It is very comfortable. There are high class boarding houses run by Miss O'Connor and Mrs. Gatmell. These are usually filled far in advance.

In Srinagar there are several agents who fit one out with everything necessary for the trip to Leh. Cockburn's (pronounced Coburne) is the largest and best. All necessary clothes and shoes for the trip can be purchased in Srinagar at reasonable cost.

Two people can travel more cheaply than three to Leh.

247

For the benefit of those who may wish to plan the trip I give the costs of my bandobast. Both supplies and equipment could have been greatly reduced with added comfort.

List of Equipment taken from Srinagar to Leh for three people. Prices cover the first six weeks.

1 10 x 10 tent for mess	3 double hot plates
2 8 x 8 tents	1 salt cellar
1 7 x 7 tent	1 pepper pot
3 pals (servants' tents)	3 soup plates
2 second-hand yakdans	3 meat plates
1 dining table	3 half plates
3 roorkie folding chairs	3 quarter plates
3 canvas cots	2 sugar bowls
3 pr. khud sticks	1 butter dish
2 water jugs	6 tumblers
2 chambers	3 egg cups
4 candle lanterns	6 teaspoons
1 meat safe	4 soup spoons
1 basin for washing pots	4 dessert spoons
1 axe	8 forks
1 chopper	8 knives
2 kettles	2 milk jugs
6 pots with lids	2 pie dishes
1 fry pan	1 cook knife
2 cook spoons	1 cook fork

Cost of above was Rs. 130 or about $49.00. This equals Rs. 21.4 or $8.00 a week. Extra was paid for each week overtime. A rupee figures at about thirty-seven cents U. S. currency.

List of supplies taken for three people. These were packed in 14 wooden boxes with hinged and padlocked lids:

12 milk	3 baked beans
12 cream	2 army rations
1 golden syrup	2 red currant jelly
12 assorted jams	2 honey
6 marmalade	1 dried herbs
2 tomato sauce	8 cocoagen
2 lbs. cooking cheese	30 lbs. sugar
2 boxes eating cheese	2 pickles
3 baking powder	6 jelly powder
18 pakts. candles	12 assorted fruits
1 prunes	4 bottled essences
12 assorted soups	1 barley
1 vermicelli	6 tomatoes
2 macaroni	1 sago
24 assorted vegetables	1 anchovy
6 ox tongue	1 tapioca
3 Keating powder	3 salmon
6 toilet paper	6 kippered herring
2 salad oil	9 sardines
2 vinegar	6 gelatine
2 salt	1 chutney
3 biscuits	2 corn flour
6 pkts. safety matches	3 paisley flour
9 sausages	24 Delhi flour
3 Quaker Oats	6 pkts. chocolate
6 Grapenuts	6 Force
½ English ham (cooked)	2 ham

2 marmite	1 Puffed Rice
7 lbs. coffee	1 ginger wine
10 lbs. tea	3 mustard
2 bottles of gin	1 curry powder
2 doz. Johnnie Walker	1 cooking sherry
2 vermouth	3 brandy
12 lime juice	

Cost of the above was Rs. 680, or about $251.00 This was ample and even too much for three people for the trips in and out and during the stay in Leh. A few fresh supplies were bought in Leh.

Excellent canned butter was sent to us from Nedou's Hotel in Srinagar. It arrived in perfect condition at various stages along the road.

The cost per pony for the one way trip of two hundred and fifty miles is Rs. 15 or about $5.55. This is paid out in small sums each day. The highest charge for each of the two longest and most trying stages was twenty-two annas per pony (this included the pony man and food for horse and himself). It was eleven annas per coolie, which also included his food. The lowest rate for any stage was nine annas for pony and five for coolie. This figures at about one anna a mile for pony with pony boy and less than that for coolies. An anna is equal to less than two and a half cents in U. S. currency. The rupee, which is sixteen annas, figures at about thirty-seven cents. This makes the cost for a coolie for the two hundred and fifty miles Rs. 7.12 or about $2.60. Half of each stage cost is always added for stop-overs between stages.

The cost of staying at dak bungalows is one rupee or

thirty-seven cents per person per day, or four annas to pitch one's tent in the surrounding grounds.

The above prices are strictly regulated by the RES RULES.

We had 25 ponies. These for the whole way in cost Rs. 375 or $138.00. This could be considerably cut.

The cost of two motor lorries and one automobile from Srinagar to Ganderbal was Rs. 30 or $11.10.

Wages: Cook-Guide Rs. 40; Bishti: Rs. 15; Sweeper: Rs. 15. This is Rs. 70 or $26.00 per month.

Each of these men was furnished with one woollen coat costing Rs. 10 ($3.70); one pair of chaplies, or sandals, Rs. 5 ($1.85); one pair of dark glasses, Rs. 1 (37 cents). There were originally four servants. Cost: Rs. 64 or $23.68.

We took in cash (in denominations of 2, 4, 8, 10 annas and Rs. 1) Rs. 600 or $222.00. All but Rs. 40 of this was spent before we reached Leh for transport, lorry, tips, bungalow charges and supplies along the road. I had forwarded Rs. 1,000 or $370.00 to an agent in Leh to hold subject to my call there. Of this Rs. 425 was spent while we were in Leh.

Before leaving Srinagar Rs. 86, or $31.82 was spent in the bazaar for petrol tins for use in boiling water for baths, dusters, sheet of tin for stove, rope, bags for grain, oil, soap, baskets, a few extra kitchen utensils, fresh vegetables. And for the servants' food which must be taken along and which is figured to cost Rs. 5, or $1.85 per man per week. It covers 20 seers (40 lbs.) rice, 4 seers (8 lbs.) dhal, 1 seer (2 lbs.) oi, 1 seer (2 lbs.) salt.

The cost of the two separate bandobasts for the return trip was approximately Rs. 500, or $185.

It would be a fair average to put the cost of the entire two and a half months for three people at Rs. 2500 or $900.00 including every expense And it must be remembered that we travelled à la Ritz. Much less equipment could be taken. Very much less food would have sufficed. This would mean fewer ponies and coolies.

GLOSSARY OF WORDS

Ahista (*pronounced asta*) .... slow
Anna......Indian currency, equal to about 2½ cents U. S.
Babu .... clerk
Bagh .... garden
Bandobast (*pronounced bundobust*) ....arrangement
Bandobast-walla .... manager of a bandobast
Behrer .... personal servant
Bishti .... water carrier
Burqua.....long robe that completely conceals Mohamedan
purdah women
Burra (*pronounced bara*) .... big, important
Chang .... drink of fermented barley water
Chaplies .... sandals
Charpoy .... native bed
Chenar .... tree peculiar to Kashmir
Chorten .... receptacle for ashes of the dead
Chota hazri .... little breakfast
Chowkidar ....keeper in dak bungalow
Chupatties.................thin cakes of unleaven bread
Dak .... stage
Durrie .... rag rug
Durzie .... tailor
Gilgits .... type of boot
Hazoor (*pronounced huzoor*) ...... literally "The Presence"
Hookah .... water pipe
Izzat .... prestige
Jelde .... hurry

Kabardar .... take care
Kassel .... Ladakhi for: "You have spoken"
Khud .... precipice
Lama .... Tibetan monk
Lamasery .... Tibetan monastery
Lucerne .... species of grass
Marg .... meadow
Nullah .... ravine
Pagri (*pronounced pugri*) .... turban
Pal .... small type of tent
Peyrak .... headdress of Ladakhi women
Pukka (*pronounced pakka*) .... first-class, excellent
Purdah .... cloistered
Rupee .... Indian coin equal to about 37c.
Sadhu .... Hindu holy man
Serai .... stable yard and quarters
Shabash .... bravo
Shawms .... long horns or trumpets
Shikara .... Kashmiri canoe
Shikari .... huntsman or guide
Skushok .... reincarnated Lama abbot
Syce .... groom
Tamasha .... celebration
Tanga .... two-wheeled native carriage
Teak .... good
Tehsildar .... village headman
Topi .... pith helmet
Yakdan .... cowhide box
Zo .... cross between yak and cow

INDEX

Acheson, Mr. J. G., Deputy Secretary for the Government of India, 9
Afghanistan, 5
Afridis, the, 62
Architecture in Leh, 212
Asoka's "Garden of Bliss," 7
Avalokita, most powerful of Buddhas, 144

Baltal, 78 ff.
Baltis, native race of, 95
"Bandobast" (native word for outfit for the trip), making a, 17 ff.; cost of, and list of supplies, 248–50, 252
Barasing, a species of deer, 241
Bathrooms in India, 79
Bazgo, ruined town of, 160–1
Benares, religious observances at, 173
Berry, Colonel A. E., 18, 20, 167, 197, 200–2, 225, 231
Berry, Mrs. A. E., 170, 171, 172, 176, 200–2, 231, 232
Birth rate in Ladakh restricted by polyandry, 123
Biscoe, Tyndale, 33
Blacker, Major, 8–9, 33
Blanc, Mt., 191
Bod Kharbu, village of, 131, 136, 233
Boiling point, effect of altitude on, 65
Brahma, 133
Brown, Lewis, "This Believing World" by, quoted, 216, 218
Buddha, 173
Buddhism, similarity between its vestments and ceremonials and those of the Catholic Church, 216 ff.; introduction of, in Tibet, 218
Buddhist prayer, a, 135
Buddhists, religious superstitions of, 133–5
Bungalows, dak, 78–9; charges for, 250–1
"Burqua," long white robes of Mohamedan purdah women, 101, 102
Butler, Samuel, 67
Butter-tea, 176, 214

Carroll, Lewis, 141
Catholic Church, similarity between its vestments and ceremonials and those of Buddhism, 216 ff.
Chamba, the Buddha who is to come, statues of, at Leh, 170, 171
Chang jugs, 167
Chasma Shahi or Giant Fountain, Kashmir, 8
"Chortens," receptacles for the ashes of the dead, 119–20, 131, 141, 142, 165, 212
"Chowkidars," in charge of dak bungalows, 79, 93
Christ, the legend of his presence in Leh, 215
Christians in Leh, 168
Cockburn's Agency, 29, 36, 247
Colossus of Rameses at Memphis, 171
Colours of mountains, 153, 158, 160
Cost of travel to Kashmir and Leh, 247 ff.
Coué, 212
Crevasses, 89, 90

255